EAT LIKE A GILMORE

Seasons

An Unofficial Cookbook
for Fans of the
GILMORE GIRLS
REVIVAL

by

KRISTI CARLSON

Skyhorse Publishing

Skyhorse Publishing books may be purchased in bulk at special discounts for sales promotion, corporate gifts, fund-raising, or educational purposes. Special editions can also be created to specifications. For details, contact the Special Sales Department, Skyhorse Publishing, 307 West 36th Street, 11th Floor, New York, NY 10018 or info@skyhorsepublishing.com.

Skyhorse® and Skyhorse Publishing® are registered trademarks of Skyhorse Publishing, Inc.®, a Delaware corporation.

Visit our website at www.skyhorsepublishing.com.

10 9 8 7 6 5 4 3 2 1

Library of Congress Cataloging-in-Publication Data is available on file.

Cover design by Tim David Kelly
Cover photos by Kristi Carlson, except author photo by Tim David Kelly

Print ISBN: 978-1-5107-7192-5

Printed in China

Graphic design and artwork by Tim David Kelly
Additional graphics by Brian Anderson
Season icons courtesy of Getty Images
All recipe photos by Kristi Carlson, except:
Italian Street Pizza, London Burger and Profiteroles by Tim David Kelly
Model for Mall Pretzels and Fluke Carpaccio: Fayth Oconnor
Models for Hot Dog Cart: Derren Harbilas and Thomas Harbilas
Rose Abdoo photo credit: Rose Abdoo
Rini Bell photo credit: Emanuela Bocse Photography
Heather Burson photo credit: Third Coast Bakery
Valerie Campbell photo credit: Janet Leahy
Leveque and Chianella photo credit: Carlo Chianella
Todd Lowe photo credit: Baque Photography

This book is dedicated to my husband, Tim David Kelly.
He gave me the initial idea to create these cookbooks,
has supported me in one hundred different ways throughout
the process, and has been a creative force behind this book.
In cookbooks and in life, Tim helps make all things possible.

CONTENTS

RECIPE GUIDE

456

Author's Note

789

Kristi Carlson

Can you remember where you were on October 19, 2015? I can. I was in a tour van, on the road with Tim's band, stopped at a gas station somewhere northwest of Jacksonville, Florida. I was sitting in the very back row, watching *Gilmore Girls* episodes on a portable DVD player, writing down food ideas for the Gilmore-based cookbook I wanted to write. Thanks, in part, to the events of that day, the book I was working on eventually became *Eat Like a Gilmore*.

Okay, so what happened on that date? At 5:30 p.m. TVLine broke the story that Netflix was bringing back *Gilmore Girls*. Rumors about a revival had been buzzing around for years, but no official announcement had ever come, until that day. My fellow fans and I had waited eight years for that announcement, and having Amy Sherman-Palladino return to make the revival carried significant meaning—the mystery of the final four words finally would be revealed.

After more than a year of frenzied anticipation within the *Gilmore Girls* community, the episodes dropped on the Friday after Thanksgiving in 2016. Like millions of others, I binged the "Winter," "Spring," "Summer," and "Fall" episodes that weekend. Watching the revival brought me back to everything I loved about the show—the characters, the small-town lifestyle, the smart, witty dialogue, and the food. It was all there. The actors were older, yes, but I was nine years older, too. It felt like reuniting with old friends after a long time apart.

Having a chance to commemorate the revival in this book has been a treat. As much as I enjoyed the revival episodes, I didn't know them the way I knew the original series. I enjoyed *A Year in the Life* but I didn't feel connected to it. Making this cookbook changed that. Researching the foods and digging into the nuances of all the scenes so I'd feel comfortable writing about them required a rewatch. It required several rewatches, actually. Immersing myself in these episodes the same way I have always immersed myself in the original series helped me grow to love the revival as much as I love the first seven seasons.

Now, I know not everyone shares my love for the revival, but, whether you love it or reject it entirely, so long as you still love food, there is something in this book for you. The eating habits of our girls did not change much. This means the diner food, the sweets, and the takeout will feel familiar to you and may even conjure up memories from the original series.

I would like to say a huge, warm "Thank you!" to some people who generously invested their time and talents in the making of this book:

To Rose Abdoo for sharing her style expertise and helping me choose a cover look, and for her delicious recipe.

To Robyn Blanchard and Ian Harbilas for allowing their tiny children be cookbook models.

To Rini Bell, Valerie Campbell and Todd Lowe for answering my request for a recipe with an enthusiastic "Yes!" and for coming through with such delicious dishes.

To Debora Leveque and Nadia and Miriam Chianella for creating their recipe half a world away and translating it from Italian to English for the book.

To Heather Burson for being the one person to contribute a recipe to each of the three cookbooks and for always offering to help me overcome my cake-baking obstacles.

To Fayth Oconnor for answering the last-minute call to model for food photographs.

To Juliet Powell for suggesting the Mall Pretzels recipe—what a great addition.

This book exists thanks to the love and encouragement I continue to receive from fellow fans. I am so grateful to everyone who has supported these cookbooks. To find kindred souls who care about this show the same way I do has been a happy surprise and feels like such a gift. Now, it's time to return to Stars Hollow.

I hope you enjoy the trip.
From my kitchen to yours,

REFERENCE GUIDE

Abbreviations
t = teaspoon

T = tablespoon

c = cup

lb = pound

oz = ounce

qt = quart

Ingredients
Butter = salted butter

Sugar = white, granulated sugar

Flour = all-purpose flour

Milk = whole milk

Vanilla = pure vanilla extract

Basic Equipment
This book assumes the reader has an oven and a refrigerator.

With regard to additional kitchen equipment, 90 percent of the recipes in this book can be made using the list below.

If you are just beginning to equip your kitchen, investing in the items on this list will enable you to cook nearly everything in this book and in most cookbooks.

If you're on a budget, many of these items can be found in good condition at thrift stores and garage sales at deep discounts.

Basic Utensils and Gadgets:
Heat-resistant rubber spatula

Wooden spoon

Slotted spoon

Wire whisk

Sharp chef's knife

Sharp serrated knife

Vegetable peeler

Grater

Strainer/fine-mesh sieve
Wire rack(s)
Citrus squeezer or juicer
Oven mitts

Stovetop Pans:
Dutch oven
Saucepans, various sizes
Frying pans, various sizes

Baking Pans:
9 x 14 baking pan
8 x 8 baking pan
Baking sheets
8-inch pie plate
8-inch cake pans x 3
Standard muffin pan

Small Appliances:
Electric mixer
Blender

Measuring Cups:
Kitchen scale
Measuring cups, dry ingredients
2-cup measuring cup, liquids
Measuring spoons
Jigger

Beverage Tools:
Coffee maker
Pitcher
Drink shaker
Frothing wand

Pastry Tools:
Candy thermometer
Rolling pin
Piping bag
Piping tips, various sizes
Biscuit cutters, various sizes

Specialized Equipment
A few recipes included in this book require specialized equipment.

Cappuccino and Ristretto:
Moka pot

Fondue:
Fondue pot
Fondue skewers

Sweet Potato Peanut Stew:
Slow cooker or multi-cooker

Brownie Bites:
Mini tart pan (12 cup)

Champagne Tango Sorbet:
Ice cream maker

GLÖGG

In 2007 when the original series ended, one of the biggest disappointments voiced by fans was that we didn't get to see Luke and Lorelai marry and have kids of their own.

Nine years later, with the airing of the revival, fans were excited to see these two make it official and start a family. Except Luke and Lorelai are both older, and each of them has a grown child already. If anything, they are entering their grandparenting years.

The "Winter" episode cuts to the chase. Right away, Luke and Lorelai discuss having a fresh kid. They visit Paris's fertility clinic. They meet a couple of breeders. Luke may or may not have gotten a handle on how the art of surrogacy works.

Ultimately, one beautiful winter afternoon, with the Town Troubadour playing in the background, they decide not to have a child together. They mark the occasion by ordering a couple of glöggs from Kirk's cart.

Ingredients:

½ c raisins (golden, brown, or a combination)

½ c orange peel without pith, cut into strips

6 cardamom pods

1–2 pieces candied or dried ginger

6 dried allspice berries

1–2 cinnamon sticks, plus more for garnish

2 anise stars

1 whole nutmeg, halved

1 T slivered raw almonds

⅔ c sugar

1–2 c brandy

1 (750ml) bottle red wine

This recipe takes multiple days to prepare.

Flavor and ferment fruits: In a 1-quart jar with a tight-fitting lid, combine the raisins, orange peel, cardamom pods, ginger pieces, allspice, cinnamon sticks, anise, nutmeg, almonds, and sugar. Mix together. Add enough brandy to cover all of the contents. Cover with lid and leave on countertop for 4 days. Once a day, give the jar a gentle shake to mix contents.

Make glögg: Pour the wine into a large saucepan, Dutch oven, or, if your name is Kirk, a copper cauldron. Add the fermented mixture from the jar. Stir to combine. Heat over medium heat for 30 minutes. If liquid begins to boil, reduce heat to a simmer for the duration. Let cool. Pour into mugs. Garnish each with a cinnamon stick. Serve.

Makes 4–6 servings

CAPPUCCINO

Paris walks into Chilton filled with confidence and power, and with an agenda: gather first-hand intel on how the school invests donations from alumni. Single-minded as she is, the minute she sees Fake Tristan, she loses it. While hiding out in their old high school bathroom, she admits to Rory that, for all of her success as a fertility guru, she still wrestles with some teenaged hang-ups. She also admits her briefcase is empty. She only brought it as a prop.

Rory enters Chilton wearing a pretty dress, ready to spend the day sharing her wisdom and giving the students some hope. The headmaster casts a dark cloud on her rosy day, however, when he offers her a cappuccino and a *job*.

Why would aspiring journalist Rory Gilmore ever take a job as a high school teacher? Suddenly she knows that he knows that she is struggling in her career. She declines both offers.

Rory, you're a Gilmore. What's going on? At least accept the cappuccino!

Ingredients:

2 T (10g) ground espresso

2 oz water

½ c milk

Cinnamon, for serving

Sugar, for serving

Brew espresso: In an espresso machine or stovetop Moka pot, add the espresso and the water. If using the espresso machine, simply turn it on and let it do its thing. If using a Moka pot, add water to the bottom and the espresso to the center "puck" area. Screw the pot together and place it on the stove, over medium heat. Remove from heat once espresso has brewed.

Scald milk: While espresso is brewing, heat the milk. In a small saucepan, add the milk and heat over medium heat. When a thin skin begins to form over the top of the milk, remove from heat.

Foam milk: Using an electronic frothing wand, or an immersion blender, froth the milk.

Assemble and serve: Pour brewed espresso into two coffee cups. Pour in milk, taking care to hold back the foam. Once espresso and milk are combined, carefully spoon foam onto the top of each beverage. Sprinkle with cinnamon and/or stir in sugar, if desired. Serve.

Makes 2 servings (or 1 Gilmore-sized serving)

RISTRETTO

During the town meeting, Taylor brings up the topic of A-list actors staying in Woodbury, throwing their money around town on extravagances like toiletries, sundresses, and three newspapers a day. Meanwhile, Stars Hollow has to make do with the B-list actors staying at The Dragonfly*, who buy nothing.

Back at the Dragonfly, Michel is clearly on Taylor's side, echoing Taylor's arguments to persuade Lorelai to make upgrades to the inn, like adding mini-fridges and a spa. He points out that the Cheshire Cat offers its A-list guests suites with mini-fridges and soaking tubs.

Hold on. Isn't the Cheshire Cat the inn where Lorelai and Rory stayed with the rose wallpaper and the fuzzy mints dinner, where the most exciting amenity was getting to ring the bell? It sounds like LaDonn either sold the place or heavily invested in upgrades over the past fifteen years!

Michel has a valid point. Even with the geographical constraints, the very least Lorelai could do is add an espresso machine to each room. Who doesn't enjoy waking up to a morning ristretto while reading their three newspapers?

Ingredients:

2 T (10 g) ground espresso

1 oz water

Sugar, for serving

Brew ristretto—espresso machine: Add water to the water receptacle of an espresso machine. Spoon the espresso into the portafilter (the "puck" area) and tamp down. Secure the portafilter into its slot. Press the brew button.

Brew ristretto—Moka pot: Using a Moka pot, add the water to the base. Add the espresso to the center filter basket ("puck" area). Screw the pot together. Place onto the stovetop, over medium heat. Once the coffee has fully brewed, remove it from heat.

Serve: Pour brewed ristretto into two espresso cups. Serve with sugar, if desired.

Makes 2 servings

*Who is the "little bird" who spilled all of the private info about the inn's guests? Michel is Suspect #1.

SANGRIA

Taylor has added a new event to the town festival schedule. It is a springtime International Food Festival featuring foods from all 195 countries (or at least fifteen). Gypsy's booth, celebrating Spain, gives us this traditional recipe for sangria.

This recipe is quick and easy to make. The night before your next get-together, spend ten minutes combining these few ingredients. The next day, serve it right out of the pitcher! Your guests will be raving.

Ingredients:

2 oranges, washed, thinly sliced,
seeds removed

1 lemon, washed, thinly sliced, seeds
removed

1 lime, washed, thinly sliced, seeds
removed

6 c sweet red wine

1 c white rum

Make sangria: In a large pitcher or beverage dispenser, combine all ingredients. Stir gently to combine liquids. Refrigerate overnight.

Serve: Pour into glasses. Garnish with slices of wine-soaked citrus. Serve.

Makes 10–12 servings

GIN MARTINI

TOWN FAVORITE

Stars Hollow has needed a vibey place to have a drink, enjoy some music, and hang out with friends for a long time. Well, forever.

During the "Summer" episode, we find out why such a place has never existed: Taylor.

His "over my dead body" commentary in response to opening a bar in town pretty clearly illustrates his views. (Of course, this makes no sense considering Stars Hollow already has a bar, Casey's.)

In rebellion against Taylor's obstruction, the townspeople have gotten together and opened a speakeasy, The Secret Bar!

With the town's trademark twinkle lights, the aged brick-wall aesthetic, the moody tunes coming from Lane and Zack, fellow townspeople at every table, and the overall clandestine vibe, doesn't this seem like the very best place to enjoy a martini?

Ingredients:

Ice

3 oz gin

1½ oz vermouth

Lemon, green olives, or pearl onions, for serving

Chill glasses: Place martini glasses in the freezer for a few minutes to chill.

Shake martini: Fill drink shaker halfway with ice. Add gin and vermouth. Shake for 30 seconds.

Make lemon twist: If using a lemon twist as garnish, wash lemon thoroughly. Use a peeler to peel only the outermost part of the rind. Avoid including any of the white pith in the peel. Use a knife to cut the peel into ½ inch strips. Twist each lemon strip around the handle of a spoon or a chopstick. These are your lemon twists!

Serve: Strain martini into chilled glass. Garnish with lemon twist by resting the curl of the twist on the edge of the glass. If using olive or onion, pierce with a toothpick or cocktail pick. Add the pick to the glass. Serve.

Makes one 4½-ounce martini

GIMLET

EMILY'S STAFF

Arriving to pick up Emily to go view Richard's newest headstone, Lorelai walks out onto the Gilmore patio to find her mother visiting with a man. This is most likely the first time in over a decade, since Richard and Emily's separation, that Lorelai has seen her mother alone with another man. Despite Jack's friendly demeanor, something about him offering Lorelai a gimlet sets off her alarm bells. She escapes into the kitchen and calls Rory to exclaim that she has a new daddy.

Lorelai need not have worried. All Emily was doing was accepting companionship and a few cocktails from an old family friend.

The gimlet is a refreshing cocktail that is easy to make in batches. It is just the sort of beverage to have on hand when friends, old and new, drop by for some companionship.

Ingredients:

¼ c grated lime zest

¾ c freshly squeezed lime juice

1 c sugar

2 c water

2–3 t citric acid

Ice

3 c vodka or gin*

Lime wedges, for garnish

Prepare lime syrup: In a medium saucepan, combine the lime zest, lime juice, sugar, water, and citric acid. Stir to combine. Over medium heat, continue to stir until the sugar and citric acid have dissolved fully. Remove from heat. Let cool. Strain through a sieve into a pitcher to remove the zest.

Make gimlets: Add ice and vodka or gin to the pitcher. Stir to combine. Pour liquid, but no ice, into glasses. Garnish each glass with a lime wedge. Serve.

*Water may be used in place of the alcohol to make a tangy, refreshing limeade.

Makes 10–12 servings

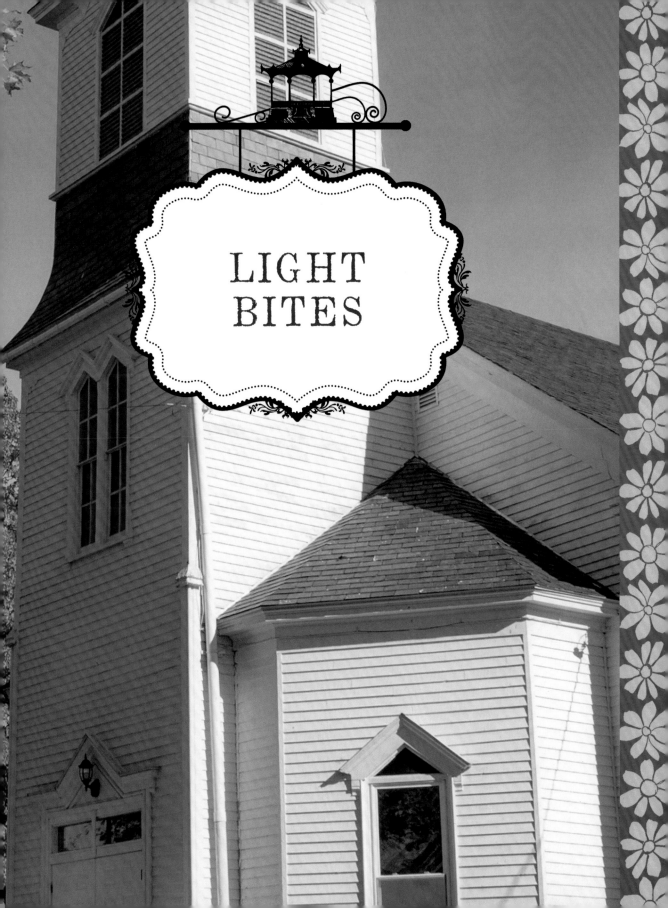

LIGHT
BITES

GARLIC BREAD

After being away for nine long years, our first view of Stars Hollow slowly drops us into the snow-white town square right after Christmas. Lorelai and Rory reunite in the gazebo, setting off a firestorm of dialogue. After a quick trip around town, they make their way back to the house. Lorelai's house is looking especially homey and welcoming in its colorful holiday lights. Even better, we find Luke in the kitchen preparing a huge "Welcome Home!" dinner, beginning with garlic bread.

All of Lorelai's carefully selected vintage pieces now serve as the backdrop for actual pots, pans, and cooking utensils. Things are different, but they are also very much the same.

Welcome home, indeed.

Ingredients:

⅓ c butter

4 cloves garlic, peeled and crushed

½ loaf French bread, freshly baked

½ c finely grated Parmesan cheese

½ t black pepper

1 t crushed red pepper flakes

2 T minced Italian flat-leaf parsley

Makes 8–10 pieces of garlic bread

Prepare oven and pan: Ensure oven rack is in the center position. Turn on broiler. Cover a baking sheet with aluminum foil. Set aside.

Make garlic butter: In a small saucepan, melt the butter over low heat. Once it has melted, add the crushed garlic. Stir occasionally. Once the edge begins to bubble, remove from heat. Let cool.

Cut the bread: Using a serrated knife, cut the half loaf of bread into two pieces like one would cut a bagel or a hamburger bun. Position the two pieces side by side, crust-side down on the foil-covered baking sheet.

Prepare the bread: Remove the garlic pieces from butter and set aside. Using a food-safe brush or a spoon, slather the melted butter onto the cut side of the bread, taking care to cover all of it. Mince the garlic pieces and distribute them, evenly, across both pieces of bread. Next, sprinkle Parmesan cheese over the bread in an even layer. Add the black pepper and crushed red pepper.

Broil: Place the baking sheet in the oven. Broil for 5–6 minutes. Once bread is golden on top, remove from oven. Sprinkle with parsley. Let cool for 5 minutes.

Serve: Cut bread into 2-inch slices. Serve.

SHRIMP & DIPS

After firing hundreds of maids during the original series, in "Winter" a miracle has happened. Emily has found someone she loves: Berta.

This recipe for Shrimp Cocktail was developed with Berta in mind. It's a fresh take on a traditional dish, layering two dips instead of one. It is suitable to serve at a funeral, yes, but please don't wait for one before you try it.

Ingredients:

Ice

6 c water

2 lemons, thinly sliced

1 orange, thinly sliced

1 lime, thinly sliced

2 T kosher salt

1 lb shrimp, raw, heads removed, deveined

2–3 limes, for serving

Red Sauce

6 oz tomatoes

3 oz red onion, peeled, quartered

2 t hot sauce, Tabasco recommended

¼ c ketchup

1 T horseradish

½ t kosher salt

Prepare ice: Fill a large bowl with ice. Place a smaller bowl on top of the ice. Set aside.

Cook shrimp: In a large saucepan, heat water. Add citrus slices and salt. Bring to a boil. Add shrimp. Once each shrimp has turned pink and floated to the top of the water, remove using a slotted spoon. Place each cooked shrimp into the bowl sitting on ice. This will prevent the shrimp from cooking further. Repeat until all shrimp has been removed from the pan. Discard the remaining contents of the pan.

Refrigerate shrimp: Once the shrimp has fully cooled, cover it with plastic wrap and refrigerate. May be stored up to 24 hours before serving.

Make red sauce: Combine all ingredients for red sauce in a blender or food processor. Blend until all large pieces have been liquified and the sauce has reached a smooth consistency. Spoon sauce into a small bowl, cover with plastic wrap, and refrigerate.

(Continued on next page)

SHRIMP & DIPS

(Continued)

Ingredients:

Green Sauce

4 oz peeled and pitted avocado, pits reserved

1 T freshly squeezed lemon juice

1 handful cilantro leaves

¼ c mayonnaise

1 jalapeño, stem and seeds removed

2 T freshly squeezed orange juice

½ teaspoon kosher salt

Make green sauce: In a medium bowl, combine all ingredients for green sauce. Use a fork to mash the avocado and to incorporate the other ingredients. Sauce should be a little chunky when finished. Spoon sauce into a small bowl. If refrigerating overnight, place the reserved avocado pits into the sauce to help prevent browning. Cover the bowl with plastic wrap. Refrigerate.

Assemble shrimp and sauces: Spoon a few tablespoons of the green sauce into a small glass dish. Wet the back of a spoon and use it to level the sauce. Use a paper towel to remove any residue on the glass above the sauce. Next, spoon in 2–3 tablespoons of the red sauce, using the back of the spoon to level it and using a paper towel to remove any residue from the glass. Arrange 6–8 shrimps around the rim of the glass, tail-side out. Garnish with a lime slice. Repeat for each serving. Serve.

Makes 2–3 shrimp cocktails

FLUKE CARPACCIO

LONDON

When we first see Rory, we see a beautiful, jet-setting young woman who has written a piece for the *New Yorker*. She spends her time traveling back and forth to London, taking lunch meetings at the club, and working on a book deal with a famous personality. She is impressive!

Of course, as the story develops, we realize Rory is homeless, in that she has moved out of her apartment and has not moved into a new one. She is having trouble nailing down any work, is involved with two men, and her self-confidence has plummeted.

At her lunch with Naomi Shropshire, though, she's the best version of herself. She's confident. She's selling herself. She's effortlessly winning over Naomi and she's not even wearing her lucky outfit (or any underwear!).

When Naomi hijacks a dish from the waiter, it's fluke carpaccio. Rory tries it and it's delicious, but is it also foreshadowing? Is this upswing in Rory's career a fluke?

Ingredients:

1½ lb fresh, deboned, skinned fluke (may substitute Mexican flounder)

1–2 limes, for garnish

Sauce

¼ c mirin

½ t sesame oil

2 T very thinly sliced green onion, white part only

¼ c freshly squeezed lime juice

1 T freshly squeezed orange juice

½–1 serrano chili, sliced paper-thin

1 t soy sauce

1 t Japanese 7 spices blend

Refrigerate fish up to 24 hours before serving: Place fish in an airtight plastic bag, removing as much air as possible before sealing. Fill a large bowl or plastic storage container half full with ice. Place the bag containing the fish into the bowl or container. Cover. Place the bowl/container in the refrigerator.

Make sauce: Combine all 8 ingredients into a medium bowl or large measuring cup. Stir to combine. Refrigerate for 2 hours before serving.

Serve: Use a sharp knife to slice the fluke into thin slices. Arrange slices on a plate. Spoon sauce over the fish. Garnish the plate with slices or wedges of fresh lime. Serve.

Makes 8–10 servings

TORTILLA ESPAÑOLA

Gypsy's got the hot hand at the International Food Festival! Not only is she serving Sangria; she's also wowing townspeople with her traditional Spanish omelet.

Serve this versatile dish hot, cold, or in between. Enjoy it for breakfast or a midday snack, or set up a booth of your own and charge your neighbors five bucks a plate (after securing proper permits, of course)!

Ingredients:

8 eggs

1 t sea salt

1 c olive oil (½ c if using a non-stick pan)

2 russet or Yukon Gold potatoes, peeled and thinly sliced

2 sweet or yellow onions, peeled, cut into ¼-inch slices

Dash of kosher salt

½ lb ham or bacon slices, cooked, cut into 1-inch pieces (optional)

2 T chopped flat-leaf parsley

Makes 8 servings

Beat eggs: Crack eggs into a medium bowl. Add sea salt. Use a fork or whisk to whip the eggs into a frothy, smooth consistency. Set aside.

Cook potatoes and onions: Heat olive oil in a large frying pan over medium-high heat. Add potatoes and onions to pan. It will seem like a lot, but will cook down. Use a slotted spatula to carefully turn the potatoes and onions as they cook.

Cook egg: Once the potatoes are golden with a slight bit of brown around the edges, give the eggs one more whip, then pour them over the potatoes and onions. Shake the pan a little bit to get the egg mixture into all of the cracks and crevices. Sprinkle kosher salt, to taste, over the entire pan. If using ham or bacon, add it to the pan now. Reduce heat to medium and cook for 10–12 minutes.

Flip tortilla: Now for the flip! You'll probably want to put on oven mitts for this. Using another frying pan of similar size, or a large plate, invert and cover the top of the potato, onion, and egg mixture. Holding the handle of the main frying pan in one hand, and the new frying pan or plate in your dominant hand, flip the omelet! Once flipped, use the spatula to gently slide the omelet back into its original frying pan. You did it!

Finish cooking: Cook the second side of the omelet over low heat for 15–20 minutes.

Serve: Slide omelet out of the frying pan and onto a cutting board. Use a large knife to cut it into wedges, like a pie. Place one wedge on each plate. Sprinkle with parsley. Serve.

CRAB BALLS

EMILY'S STAFF

When Emily hosts a meeting on her patio for her DAR ladies, her impatience with them begins to show. She is more assertive with them. Her exasperation at their lack of diligence is thinly veiled. Of course, this episode is nothing compared to her epic outburst a few months later, when she turns "bullshit!" into a freedom chant, and finally bids "adieu" to the DAR.

Leaving the DAR is a small part of the bigger picture. After Richard's death, Emily transforms her entire life. Gone are the endless social engagements, the St. John suits, and even the impressively large house. Watching Emily discard the rigid structure of her old life and phase into a softer, simpler persona raises the question "Was she ever true to herself while Richard was alive, or did she live to please him?"

By the "Fall" episode, Emily has fully evolved into a new version of herself and, shockingly, is far more like Lorelai than the old Emily ever was.

Ingredients:

2 russet potatoes, peeled and cubed

1 t salt

1–2 eggs

2 c finely grated Parmesan cheese

4 T butter

½ t white pepper

⅛ t cayenne pepper

3–4 T milk or oat milk

10 oz lump crabmeat or imitation crab, in thin strands

2–3 oz Havarti cheese, cut into 24 (½-inch) cubes

Oil, shortening, or additional butter to grease pan

Boil potatoes: Place potato cubes in a medium saucepan. Add enough water to cover potatoes. Add salt. Bring to a boil over medium-high heat. Reduce heat to medium, and continue to boil for 8–10 minutes. Test potatoes for doneness by poking a fork into a cube. As soon as the fork goes easily into the cube, remove from heat and drain water.

Prep oven and pan: Ensure the oven rack is in the center position. Preheat oven to 375°F. Cover a large baking sheet with aluminum foil, parchment paper, or a silicone mat. Set aside.

Prep eggs and Parmesan cheese: Crack eggs into a small bowl. Whisk with a fork until yolks and whites are fully combined. Set aside. Pour Parmesan cheese into another small bowl. Set aside.

Mash potatoes: Add butter, white pepper, cayenne pepper, and milk or oat milk to potatoes. Use an electric hand mixer to combine ingredients and mash the potatoes. Continue to beat until potatoes have reached a smooth yet sturdy consistency.

(Continued on next page)

CRAB BALLS

(Continued)

Mix in crab: Fold the crabmeat into the potatoes, continuing to mix until it's evenly distributed.

Roll balls: Fill 1½-inch scooper with mashed potatoes. Place one cube of Havarti cheese into center of the potato ball. Release potato ball, then roll it into a perfect ball by hand, taking care to fully cover the cheese. Roll the ball in egg mixture, then roll in Parmesan cheese, fully covering. Place on tray. Repeat until all potatoes have been rolled.

Bake potato balls: Place baking sheet in oven. Bake for 15 minutes. Remove from oven. Let cool. Serve.

Makes 24 (1¾-inch) balls

FONDUE

TOWN FAVORITE

During the "Summer" episode, outside the movie theater, there is a sign banning fondue, of all things. Not food. Just fondue. Isn't this an oddly specific food to mention? Then again, this is Stars Hollow.

Is it a stretch to imagine Lorelai waltzing in to watch a movie, carrying with her a pot of melted cheese? Not really. The question is, which type of fondue would she choose?

The clear answer is . . . Nacho Cheese Fondue.

This recipe will not make a fancy Sookie fondue, nor does it require a $60 investment in fine cheeses. This recipe is for a quick, easy, nacho-cheesy fondue created specifically with Lorelai in mind.

If you prefer a more nuanced Luke-style fondue flavor, swap out half of the cheddar cheese for mild Swiss, and omit the green chilis.

Ingredients:

16 oz cold beer, pilsner or nonalcoholic pilsner, Coors Light recommended

1½ t cornstarch

20 oz medium or sharp cheddar cheese, shredded

1 T sodium citrate*

2 t freshly squeezed lemon juice

1 t Dijon mustard

1 (4-oz) can green chilis, diced, with liquids, *optional*

*Sodium citrate is a naturally occurring emulsifier. It is what gives nacho cheese its smooth consistency. The food-grade version is available for purchase online.

Note: Buy the cheese for this recipe in a block and grate it at home. Pre-grated cheese will result in a clumpy fondue.

Dissolve cornstarch: Measure cold beer in a clear measuring cup or jar. (Beer must be cold for cornstarch to dissolve.) Add cornstarch. Beer will foam slightly. Using a fork, gently stir until cornstarch has fully dissolved.

Heat beer and melt cheese: Pour beer into a medium saucepan. Over medium-high heat, bring to a simmer. Bubbles will begin to appear around the edge. Add cheese. Stir until cheese is fully melted. Cheese may appear clumpy or stringy at this stage. Stir in sodium citrate. Continue stirring. Bring mixture to a boil. Boil for 2 minutes. As it boils, continue stirring.

Add remaining ingredients: Once cheese has reached a smooth, even consistency, stir in lemon juice, mustard, and green chilis, if using. Reduce heat. Simmer for 2–3 minutes. Pour into fondue pot. Light a heat source under the pot.

Serve: Serve with tortilla chips, bread, soft pretzels (page 33), meatballs (page 105), cut vegetables, and/or cooked curly pasta.

Makes 1 quart

MALL PRETZELS

TOWN FAVORITE

While out in nature, in the middle of California, Lorelai finally gets in touch with her emotions. The death of her father fully hits her. At that moment, she calls her mother. When a groggy Emily answers from bed, Lorelai dives right in. She tells the story of her thirteenth birthday when Richard happened to find her at the mall. She was wearing Emily's forbidden green beaded top, crying her eyes out over being dumped by her boyfriend, hungry, wishing she had money to buy a pretzel.

She tells of the way Richard's demands to know why she wasn't in school gave way to a rare moment of fatherly nurturing. Not only did he buy her the pretzel she wanted, he also spent the rest of the afternoon with her and took her to the movies.

It was the type of memory Emily had been waiting for Lorelai to share since the funeral, and it was perfect.

Ingredients:

1 c water, warm but not hot

1 packet active dry yeast (approx. ¼ oz.)

1 t sugar

2 c flour

½ t salt

½ t baking powder

2 c warm water

2 T baking soda

½ c melted butter

Coarse salt, *optional*

Prepare oven and pan: Ensure oven rack is positioned in the center. Preheat oven to 400°F. Cover a large baking sheet with parchment paper, aluminum foil, or a silicone mat. Set aside.

Bloom yeast: Pour 1 cup warm water into a small bowl. Add yeast. Sprinkle in the sugar. Don't stir. Let the mixture sit for 10 minutes. Look for bubbles which will indicate the yeast is active. If there are no bubbles, and no visible activity, discard mixture and begin again using new yeast.

Mix dough: In a medium bowl, mix flour, salt, and baking powder. Use a fork to stir in the yeast mixture until a ragged dough is formed. Turn the dough and any remaining flour onto the counter and knead the dough together, until it is more fully formed. Incorporate the remaining flour along the way.

(Continued on next page)

MALL PRETZELS

(Continued)

Proof dough: Use a fresh dish towel or invert a large bowl to cover the dough. Leave it to rise for 90 minutes.

Knead dough: Once dough has risen, press it down in the center, then gently pull each corner into the center. Sprinkle the counter with flour then knead the dough by hand for 15–20 turns.

Assemble pretzels: Sprinkle a thin layer of flour onto the counter again. Use a rolling pin to roll out dough into a rectangle measuring 20 inches wide by 12 inches deep. Use a pizza cutter or a knife to cut dough horizontally into twelve 20-inch strips. To form the pretzel shape, form a U shape, then bring each end down, diagonally, to the opposite side. Once both ends are down, twist them once or twice, then layer them onto the base of the U, and press them in, gently.

Dip pretzels: In a large bowl, combine 2 cups of warm water with 2 tablespoons of baking soda. Stir until baking soda has dissolved. One by one, dip each pretzel for 10 seconds before removing and placing onto the baking sheet.

Bake pretzels: Once all pretzels are on the baking sheet, leave them to rise for 20–30 minutes. Place in the oven and bake for 10–12 minutes.

Serve: Remove pan from oven. Brush pretzels with melted butter and sprinkle with coarse salt, if using. Serve.

Makes 12 pretzels

FAT-FREE GRANOLA

During the "Fall" episode, Sookie returns! Lorelai is thrilled and a little surprised. They hug. They laugh. They reminisce. Sookie sprays frosting across the entire kitchen.

Just as it starts to feel like old times, Michel appears, furious with Sookie. He rattles on about what a wreck Lorelai has been without her, blaming Sookie for deserting them.

Sookie is nonplussed. She has too many years of experience dealing with Michel's tantrums to let this one get to her. Plus, she knew he'd behave this way, so she brought his favorite fat-free granola with her to appease him, tons of it. Her trick works. The granola is just the shiny object needed to get Michel out of the kitchen, so she and Lorelai can resume their heartfelt reunion.

Sookie may not be around much, but it's still her kitchen.

Ingredients:

2 c uncooked rolled oats

1 c puffed corn

1 c puffed rice

1 c puffed millet

1 c quinoa flakes

¾ c plain nonfat yogurt

¼ c brown sugar

3 T maple syrup

1 t vanilla extract

2 t cinnamon

½ t sea salt

½ c diced dried apricots

½ c halved dried tart cherries

¼ c freeze-dried blueberries

¼ c diced dried pineapple

Makes 6 cups

Prepare oven and pan: Ensure oven rack is positioned in center of oven. Preheat oven to 225°F. Cover a large baking sheet with a silicone mat or parchment paper. Set aside.

Combine grains: In a large bowl combine oats, puffed corn, puffed rice, puffed millet and quinoa flakes. Set aside.

Prepare yogurt sauce: In a small bowl, combine yogurt, brown sugar, maple syrup, and vanilla. Stir to combine.

Mix yogurt sauce into grains: Fold the yogurt sauce into the grains until fully incorporated. Spoon grains onto baking sheet in a single layer. Sprinkle grains with cinnamon and sea salt.

Bake grains: Place baking sheet in oven. Bake for 30 minutes. Turn off oven. Keep baking sheet in oven with door closes for 10 minutes. Remove baking sheet from oven. Let cool for 10 minutes.

Make granola: Mix the dried fruits into the baked grains. Store in ziplock bags or a bowl with a tight-fitting lid.

Serve: Serve as a stand-alone snack, with milk as a cereal, or as a topping for yogurt.

SANDWICHES, PIZZAS & TACOS

TATER TOT TACOS

The Gilmore girls still really love a Tater Tot. Even when they've already eaten tacos, presumably from Al's, and are about to sit down to a massive meal Luke has prepared from scratch, Lorelai dares to try to add Tater Tots to the menu. Rory backs her up, but Luke keeps her at bay by throwing a small fit and refusing to make anything else. During the squabble, however, a wonderfully Gilmore-esque idea is born—Tater Tots in a taco!

Ingredients:

½ bag frozen Tater Tots
(about 3 cups or 50 tots)

1 t smoked paprika

1 t chili powder

½ t cumin, ground

Kosher salt, to taste

Black pepper, to taste

1 T olive oil

1 c finely chopped red onion

1 jalapeño, stemmed, seeded, and diced

2 cloves garlic, peeled and minced

1 (15-oz) can black beans, drained and rinsed

½ c chopped cilantro

½–1 t kosher salt

6–8 corn tortillas

Iceberg lettuce, chopped, for serving

Tomato, finely chopped, for serving

Cheese (cheddar, colby, Monterey Jack or a mix), shredded, for serving

Chipotle Cream

1 c crema, sour cream or plain Greek yogurt, for serving

2 T chipotle sauce

2 t freshly squeezed lime juice

Prepare oven and pan: Ensure oven rack is in the center position. Preheat oven to 450°F. Cover a large baking sheet with aluminum foil, parchment paper, or a silicone mat. Set aside.

Bake Tater Tots: Combine Tater Tots, smoked paprika, chili powder, cumin, salt, and pepper in a large ziplock bag or a covered bowl. Gently shake until all seasoning is attached to the tots. Carefully pour tots out onto the baking sheet, arranging them in a single layer. Place the pan in the oven. Bake for 20–25 min or according to instructions on the package.

(Continued on next page)

TATER TOT TACOS

(Continued)

Prepare filling: In a large frying pan, heat the olive oil over medium-high heat. When oil is hot, add the red onion, jalapeño, and garlic. Sauté until onions are translucent. Add beans, cilantro, and salt. Reduce heat to medium-low. Continue to sauté, stirring occasionally, until beans are heated through. Once Tater Tots are finished baking, remove them from the oven. Add them to the bean mixture, taking care not to smash or break the tots. This is your taco filling.

Heat tortillas: Cover the tortillas in a damp paper towel. Heat them in the microwave on high for 2 minutes. Leave them in the microwave for an additional minute, without heat. Remove them from microwave. Scoop a portion of filling into each tortilla.

Make chipotle cream: In a small bowl, combine all ingredients. Stir to combine.

Assemble tacos: Fill each taco with lettuce, tomatoes and cheese, as desired. Top with a drizzle of chipotle cream. Serve.

Makes 6–8 tacos

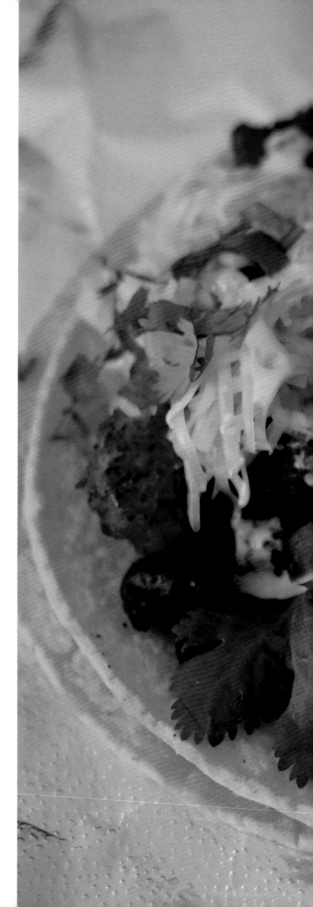

BLT SANDWICH

Now that Kirk and Lulu are proud pet parents of Petal, their tiny pink pig, Kirk's newfound interest in the welfare of pigs is creating a bit of a crisis for him. When he sees the whole pig being roasted in the town square, he flips! He lays into Phan, asking him how he could be so cruel.

Luke overhears the exchange and gently reminds Kirk that the BLT sandwich he eats at the diner contains bacon, which comes from pigs. At that moment, for the first time, Kirk draws the connection between eating bacon and caring for his beloved pet.

How does Kirk resolve this moral conflict? Does he stop eating bacon? Perhaps, but even if Kirk never eats bacon again, Luke's Diner will continue making its BLT sandwich. Although, thankfully, Luke doesn't say "dead pig" while serving it.

Ingredients:

6 slices thick-cut bacon (may substitute vegan bacon)

1 T butter

2 slices soft wheat, white, or brown bread

Mustard, to taste

Mayonnaise, to taste

2–4 leaves iceberg or leaf lettuce

2 slices tomato

Fry bacon: In a large frying pan or on a griddle, fry bacon slices over medium-high heat, 2–3 minutes per side. Remove bacon and place on a paper towel to collect excess grease.

Toast bread: Pour off excess grease from pan into a bowl or jar for disposal later. Add butter to pan and melt over medium heat. Place bread in pan to sop up the melted butter and to toast. Once the bread turns a golden color on the toasted side, remove it from the pan. Place on a plate.

Assemble sandwich: Coat soft side of bread with mustard and mayonnaise, as desired. Arrange bacon, lettuce and tomato on one piece of bread. Flip over other side of bread and place atop the tomato. Cut sandwich in half. Serve.

Makes 1 sandwich

SAMMIES

It seems lunch at the Dragonfly is more of a problem than ever with Sookie gone. Michel does his best to find a fun, hip solution by inviting some of the most popular, well-known chefs to host pop-up lunches.

Though it seems Lorelai approved the idea for the pop-ups when Michel pitched it, when the lunches take place, she blatantly obstructs them.

Under normal circumstances, having a famous chef come in and create signature food each week sounds like something Lorelai would love. So watching her awkwardly fire chef after chef (even Queen Ina herself!) using a different excuse each time makes it clear she is in denial about Sookie.

It also makes it seem like Lorelai is turning into Emily, firing everyone. Instead of maids, it's chefs.

PROSCIUTTO PROVOLONE PANINI

Ingredients:

2 thin slices Italian bread

1 T fig jam

2 thin slices prosciutto

1–2 slices provolone cheese

1 T butter

Assemble sandwich: Lay out two slices of bread. Spread fig jam on each slice. On one slice, pile the prosciutto and provolone. Flip the other piece of bread over and place it atop the provolone.

Toast sandwich: In a small frying pan, heat a pat of butter (½ T) over medium-high heat. Once it has melted, place the assembled sandwich in the butter. Allow sandwich to toast for 2–3 minutes. Using a spatula, remove sandwich from pan. Heat the second pat of butter. Once it has melted, return the sandwich to the pan, with the untoasted side down. Toast for an additional 2 minutes. Turn off heat. Allow sandwich to remain in pan for 2–3 minutes more.

Serve: Remove sandwich from pan. Cut in half. Serve.

Each recipe makes 1 sandwich

(Continued on next page)

SAMMIES

(Continued)

REUBEN

Ingredients:

1–2 T Russian dressing

2 slices rye or marble rye bread

3–4 slices corned beef

¼ c sauerkraut

1–2 slices Swiss cheese

1 T butter

Russian Dressing

2 T mayonnaise

1 T ketchup

2 t dill relish

1 t grated white onion

1 t freshly squeezed lemon juice

1 t Worcestershire sauce

Prepare Russian dressing: Combine mayonnaise, ketchup, relish, onion, lemon juice, and Worcestershire sauce in a small bowl. Stir with a fork until fully combined.

Assemble sandwich: Place two slices of rye bread flat on a counter or cutting board. Using a knife or spoon, spread Russian dressing on each slice. Top one slice with the corned beef, sauerkraut, and Swiss cheese. Flip the other slice over and place atop the Swiss cheese.

Toast sandwich: In a small frying pan, heat a pat of butter (½ T) over medium-high heat. Once it has melted, place the assembled sandwich in the butter. Allow sandwich to toast for 2–3 minutes. Using a spatula, remove sandwich from pan. Heat the second pat of butter. Once it has melted, return the sandwich to the pan, with the untoasted side down. Toast for an additional 2 minutes. Turn off heat. Allow sandwich to remain in pan for 2–3 minutes more.

Serve: Remove sandwich from pan. Cut in half. Place remaining Russian dressing in a ramekin and serve with sandwich for dipping.

To make the lighter "Rachel" version of this sandwich, substitute turkey for the corned beef, and coleslaw (page 84) for the sauerkraut.

TURKEY BRIE

Ingredients:

2 slices sourdough bread

2 T cranberry sauce

¼ t Dijon mustard

2–3 slices turkey breast

1–2 slices Brie cheese, with or without rind

1 T butter

CAPRESE

Ingredients:

2 slices focaccia bread

1 t balsamic vinegar

½ t Italian seasoning

3–4 slices fresh Roma tomato

1 chicken cutlet (page 89), fully cooked (optional)

1–2 slices mozzarella cheese

3–4 leaves fresh basil

1 T olive oil

Assemble sandwich: Lay out two slices of bread. Place cranberry sauce in a small bowl. Mix in Dijon mustard. Spread cranberry Dijon sauce on each slice. On one slice, pile the turkey breast and Brie. Flip the other piece of bread over and place it atop the Brie.

Toast sandwich: In a small frying pan, heat a pat of butter (½ T) over medium-high heat. Once it has melted, place the assembled sandwich in the butter. Allow sandwich to toast for 2–3 minutes. Using a spatula, remove sandwich from pan. Heat the second pat of butter. Once it has melted, return the sandwich to the pan, with the untoasted side down. Toast for an additional 2 minutes. Turn off heat. Allow sandwich to remain in pan for 2–3 minutes more.

Serve: Remove sandwich from pan. Cut in half. Serve.

Assemble sandwich: Lay out two slices of bread. Lightly brush balsamic vinegar on both slices, then sprinkle with Italian seasoning. On one slice, pile the tomato slices, chicken cutlet, if using, mozzarella, and basil leaves. Flip the other piece of bread over and place it atop the basil.

Toast sandwich: In a small frying pan, heat ½ tablespoon of olive oil over medium-high heat. Once the oil is hot, place the assembled sandwich in the oil. Allow sandwich to toast for 2–3 minutes. Using a spatula, remove sandwich from pan. Heat the remaining oil. Return the sandwich to the pan, with the untoasted side down. Toast for an additional 2 minutes. Turn off heat. Allow sandwich to remain in pan for 2–3 minutes more.

Serve: Remove sandwich from pan. Cut in half. Serve.

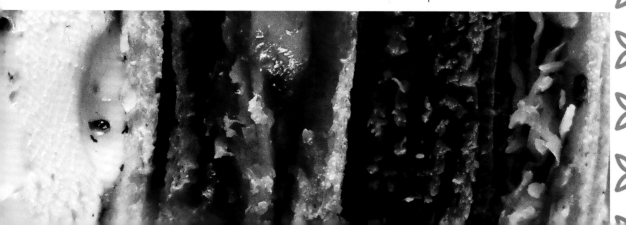

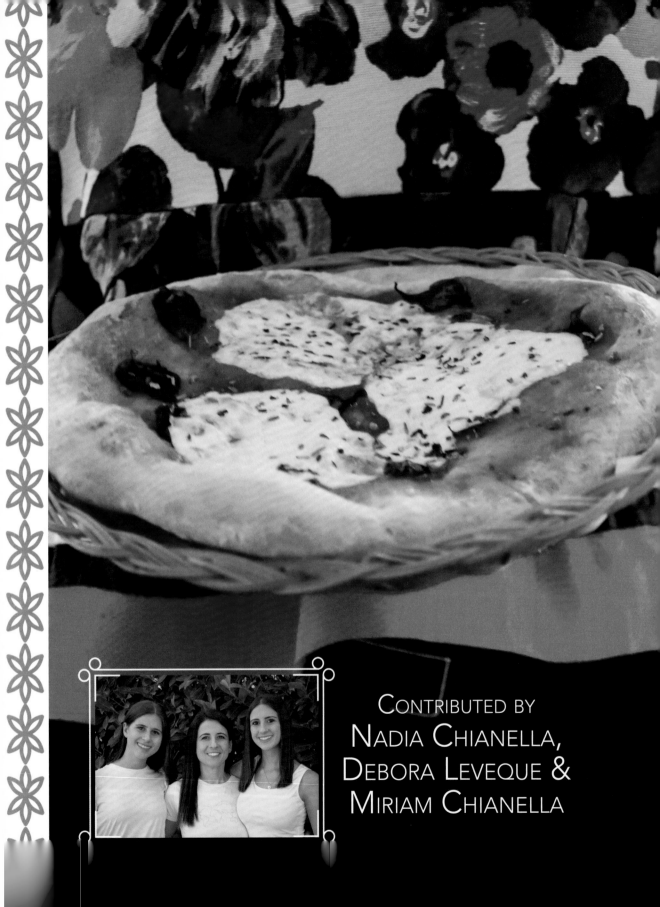

CONTRIBUTED BY
NADIA CHIANELLA,
DEBORA LEVEQUE &
MIRIAM CHIANELLA

ITALIAN STREET PIZZA

"True Neapolitan pizza is usually soft after it is baked. This is because, in Napoli, they use wood ovens. Considering most people don't have a wood oven at home, this version will be more crisp, but still delicious. Buon appetito!"

—Debora Leveque, Nadia Chianella, and Miriam Chianella

Ingredients:

Pizza Dough

2 c (500g) flour

1½ t salt

1½ c (350g) room-temperature water

1 packet active dry yeast (approx. ¼ ounce)

Pinch sugar

Pizza Sauce

6 T store-bought pizza sauce

Salt

Olive oil

8 oz mozzarella cheese, packed in water, drained 30 minutes before use, sliced thinly

18–21 leaves fresh basil

The preparation must begin the night before you want to eat pizza.

Put the flour in a large bowl. Add salt. Make a hole in the middle. Add water, yeast and sugar. Mix the liquid well and start to knead with a wooden spoon. The dough should be very soft and gooey. Eliminate the biggest lumps, by hand if you prefer. Cover the bowl with cling wrap and then rest in the fridge overnight.

Next morning the dough should be elastic enough. Spread some flour on the countertop and expand the dough by hand. Stretch it as much as possible, to make it as thin as a bedsheet, but be careful not to make any holes. At this point, fold it, bringing the right edge to the middle of the dough, then bring the left edge onto the right one. Bring the bottom edge to the middle and the top one onto the bottom edge. Stretch out the dough again, then repeat the folding process. Finally, make a ball with the dough by gathering all of the edges underneath. Close it tightly on the bottom. Cover it and put it in the fridge again.

About 5 hours before baking the pizzas, remove the dough from the fridge. Divide the dough into 3 equal portions and form 3 balls. Be careful to close them tightly on the bottom. Spread some flour in an airtight container and put the balls in it. Let them rest out of the fridge. Don't put them close to each other. If you don't have a container large enough for all three, you can use three different containers.

(Continued on next page)

ITALIAN STREET PIZZA

(Continued)

Preheat the oven to 450°F. While the oven is heating, start stretching the first pizza on a floured surface. Stretch it from the center outward, shaping it by hand into a circle with a thick outer edge, while making the center part of the dough very thin.

Grease a round baking tray (diameter of at least 12 inches) with very little oil. Put the pizza on the baking tray. Be careful not to make any holes. Season the middle with pizza sauce, salt, and oil. Put the baking tray in the oven on the lower rack for 5 minutes, then remove the baking tray from the oven. Add mozzarella and basil leaves. Put the pizza on the top rack of the oven for 5 minutes. The first pizza should be ready and you can bake the next one.

Makes 3 (12-inch) pizzas

Debora Leveque is mother to Miriam and Nadia Chianella. They are Italian and live in Tuscany.

Debora has loved Gilmore Girls since the TV series first aired. In 2018, the three of them watched it together, because, the year before, they had been in "Stars Hollow" on the Warner Brothers lot. In 2020 Nadia received the first Eat Like a Gilmore cookbook. Cooking from the book as a family was a nice way to spend the months of lockdown.

Their dream is to return to Warner Brothers. They also would love to meet some actors from Gilmore Girls. Connect with them on Instagram: @deboraleveque, @nadia_chianella, and @miriam_chianella

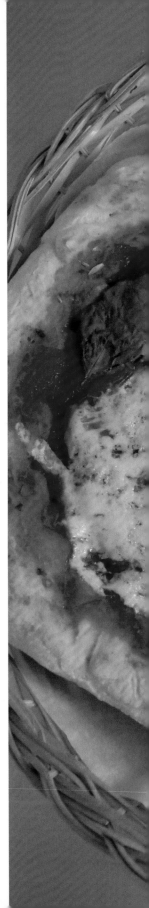

FINGER SANDWICHES

Rory arrives at the house just as Emily's DAR luncheon is wrapping up. As the ladies leave, Rory and Emily stroll into the living room together. Rory stops in her tracks when she sees a television. Emily acts like it's perfectly normal, but is it?

We've seen Emily watch television before, like the time she tortured Rory with a ballroom dancing marathon, but we have never, never, seen a television in the living room of the Gilmore house.

First, she's reading trendy books and asking if each of her belongings brings her joy, while wearing denim and a vintage T-shirt. Now she's watching television in the living room. She's also eating her meals in the living room, using a TV tray. All of this behavior is par for the course for Lorelai, but for Emily?

Wait, is Emily *turning into* Lorelai?

Something to ponder while reclining on the sofa with some finger sandwiches.

CORONATION CHICKEN

Ingredients:

½ lb cooked and shredded skinless chicken breast

2 T mayonnaise

½ t ground turmeric

¼ t ground cinnamon

⅛ t ground coriander

2 T mango chutney

2 T golden raisins

8 slices fresh white bread

3 T room-temperature butter, *optional*

Mango Chutney

2 c diced fresh or frozen mango

½ c diced red onion

¼ c sugar

3 cloves garlic, peeled and minced

1½ T peeled and minced fresh ginger

1 serrano pepper, stems and seeds removed, minced, *optional*

2 T sherry

½ t curry powder

¼ t salt

Prepare the mango chutney: In a small saucepan, combine mango, red onion, sugar, garlic, ginger, pepper, sherry, curry powder, and salt. Gently stir to combine. Bring to a boil over medium-high heat. Reduce heat to low, cover the pan, and simmer for 20 minutes. Remove from heat, stir, and let cool for 1 hour.

(Continued on next page)

FINGER SANDWICHES (Continued)

Prepare Coronation Chicken: In a medium bowl, combine chicken, mayonnaise, spices, mango chutney, and raisins. Stir to combine. Cover the bowl with its lid or plastic wrap. Refrigerate for 1 hour before using. Store the excess mango chutney in an airtight container in the refrigerator.

Assemble sandwiches: Lay out 3 slices of bread. If using butter, spread a light layer on each slice. Spread ⅓ of the Coronation Chicken onto each slice. Lay out the remaining 3 bread slices. Butter each slice, if using, then turn the slices over and use them to cover each sandwich.

Cut sandwiches: Use a sharp, serrated knife to carefully cut the crusts off the sandwich, leaving a perfectly rectangular sandwich with no crust. Cut the sandwich into 4 equal pieces. Repeat this for each sandwich. Serve.

Makes 10–12 finger sandwiches

PARIS HAM & CHEDDAR

Ingredients:

6 slices fresh white bread

3 T room-temperature butter, *optional*

9 slices Paris ham

3 slices cheddar cheese

12 paper-thin slices apple, Granny Smith preferred

1–2 T English, Dijon, or yellow mustard

Assemble sandwiches: Lay out 3 slices of bread. If using butter, spread a light layer on each slice. Pile 3 slices of ham on each. Top each with 1 slice of cheese, then 4 slices of apple. Lay out the remaining 3 bread slices. Butter each slice, if using. Spread mustard on each slice then turn the slices over and use them to cover each sandwich.

Cut sandwiches: Use a sharp, serrated knife to carefully cut the crusts off the sandwich, leaving a perfectly rectangular sandwich with no crust. Cut the sandwich into 4 equal pieces. Repeat this for each sandwich. Serve.

Makes 12 finger sandwiches

ROAST BEEF WITH HORSERADISH CREAM

Ingredients:

1 batch horseradish cream

8 slices fresh white bread

3 T room-temperature butter, *optional*

6 slices roast beef

Horseradish cream

4 oz room-temperature cream cheese

2 T prepared horseradish

2 t freshly squeezed lemon juice

½–1 t kosher salt

½ t cracked black pepper

Prepare the horseradish cream: In a small bowl, combine cream cheese, horseradish, lemon juice, salt and pepper. Use a fork to gently smash the ingredients into the cream cheese, then continue to incorporate the ingredients until a smooth spread has formed.

Assemble sandwiches: Lay out 3 slices of bread. If using butter, spread a light layer on each slice. Spread one third of the horseradish cream onto each slice. Pile 2 slices of roast beef on each. Lay out the remaining 3 bread slices. Butter each slice, if using, then turn the slices over and use them to cover each sandwich.

Cut sandwiches: Use a sharp, serrated knife to carefully cut the crusts off the sandwich, leaving a perfectly rectangular sandwich with no crust. Cut the sandwich into 4 equal pieces. Repeat this for each sandwich. Serve.

Makes 12 finger sandwiches

EGG & WATERCRESS

Ingredients:

6 slices white bread, fresh

6 eggs, large

Water

Ice

3 T mayonnaise

3 T watercress leaves, no stems, chopped (measure after chopping)

Kosher salt, to taste

Cracked black pepper, to taste

3 T room-temperature butter, *optional*

Boil eggs: Arrange eggs in one layer on the bottom of a saucepan. Fill pan with enough water to cover eggs. Over medium-high heat, bring water to a boil. Boil eggs for 8 minutes. Immediately drain water and cover eggs with cold water. Add ice. Soak eggs in ice water for 10 minutes.

Make egg salad: Peel and cut each egg in half. Then cut each half into 4 equal wedges. Next, cut each wedge in half, making sure to keep some yolk in each piece. Place egg wedges into a bowl. Top with mayonnaise, watercress, salt, and pepper. Gently mix together only until combined.

(Continued on next page)

FINGER SANDWICHES

(Continued)

Assemble sandwiches: Lay out 3 slices of bread. If using butter, spread a light layer on each slice. Spread one third of the egg mixture onto each slice. Use the remaining bread slices to cover each sandwich (butter each slice first, if using).

Cut sandwiches: Use a sharp, serrated knife to carefully cut the crusts off the sandwich, leaving a perfectly rectangular sandwich with no crust. Cut the sandwich into 4 equal pieces. Repeat this for each sandwich. Serve.

Makes 12 finger sandwiches

FRENCH BREAD PIZZA

Throughout the revival Lorelai has a lot going on. Her father has recently died. She has had to sit through soul-sucking therapy sessions with Emily. She's running the inn alone without her partner, Sookie. She and Luke have only recently decided whether or not to have a kid. Now she's mulling over Rory's bombshell plan to write a book about the intimate details of their lives. Plus, she's worrying over Michel's pending resignation. It is too much.

At Taylor's request, Lorelai goes to hear the new solo for the musical. When she walks into Miss Patty's studio and hears the song, all of the pressures in her life hit her at once, and she realizes she is not unbreakable.

She knows she has to do something drastic, or else she may lose it.

Two days later, she's in California, drinking wine and eating French bread pizza with women she just met, trying to quiet all of the noise in her life, hoping she can find herself.

Ingredients:

1 (15-oz) can tomato sauce

½ t olive oil

1 t dried oregano (double if using fresh)

1 T freshly squeezed lemon juice

¼ t kosher salt

16 oz mozzarella cheese, grated

Pepperoni, sliced

Begin this recipe by preparing the Garlic Bread recipe on page 17. Once the bread has been removed from the oven and sprinkled with parsley, proceed with this recipe.

Prepare oven: Reduce oven setting to 350°F.

Make sauce: Add tomato sauce, olive oil, oregano, lemon juice, and salt to a medium bowl. Stir to combine.

Assemble pizzas: Spoon sauce onto the garlic breads, adding as much or as little as you prefer. Top with cheese, again using as much as you prefer. Arrange the pepperoni pieces on top of cheese.

Bake: Return the baking sheet to the oven. Bake for 5 minutes. Turn on the broiler. Broil for 1 minute. Remove the baking sheet from the oven and let cool.

Serve: Use a serrated knife to cut into 2-inch slices. Serve.

Makes 4–6 servings

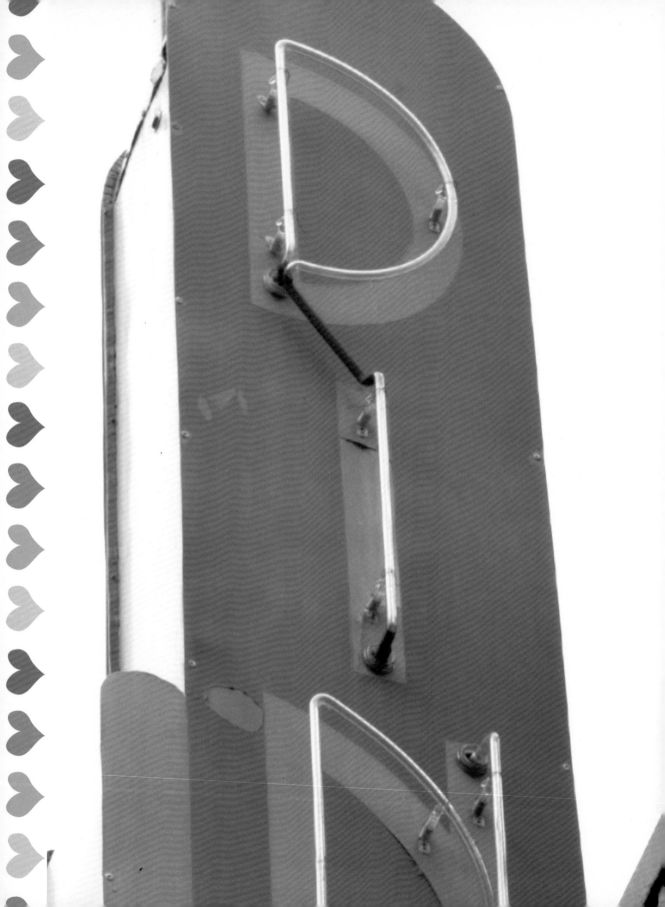

BURGERS, FRIES & DOGS

LONDON BURGER

In a luxurious London apartment, we see Rory retelling the story of her lunch with Naomi, going into great detail, but who is she telling?

She feels at home there. She's wearing an oversized T-shirt and leggings, flinging herself onto the sofa while she keeps talking, but where is she? Is this her apartment? Is she staying with a friend?

Logan walks into the room. It's Logan's apartment. Hey, it's probably Logan's T-shirt.

Logan is living in London, working for his father's company. So not a lot has changed. Except Logan has a fiancé.

We thought stealing someone else's cheeseburger was going to be the worst thing Rory did that day, but no. She's sleeping with someone else's man. Again. Rory is the other woman. Again.

Ingredients:

8–10 shallots, peeled (cut large shallots in half)

¾ c olive oil

2 sprigs fresh thyme

1 lb premium ground beef

2 t kosher salt

1 t cracked black pepper

6 T butter, *divided*

English mustard, to taste

Stilton cheese, thinly sliced

2 eggs

2 brioche buns

2 slices beefsteak tomato

Roast shallots: Preheat oven to 400°F. Place shallots in a small baking dish or large ramekin. Add olive oil and thyme. Put a baking sheet or aluminum foil under the baking dish to catch any drips or splatters. Place in the oven and roast for 30 min. Remove from oven. Keep shallots in oil until they are needed, to retain heat.

Prepare hamburger patties: Separate ground beef into two ½ pound balls. Roll each ball by hand, then flatten each to ½ inch thickness. Cup one patty with hands, from both sides and gently press in to make it round, with no cracks around the edge. Repeat for each patty. Sprinkle ½ teaspoon of kosher salt and ¼ teaspoon of black pepper onto each side of each patty. Gently press salt and pepper into each patty before turning it over.

Cook hamburgers: Place a large frying pan on the stove over high heat. Once the pan is hot, add 2 tablespoons of butter. Once it has melted, add the patties, leaving a little space between them. Cook the patties on one side for 3 minutes. Using a spatula, flip each patty. Cook the other side of the patties for 2–3 minutes more. Use the spatula to remove the patties from the pan, and place them on a plate, clean cutting board, or wire rack. While the patties rest, top each one with 1 to 2 thin slices of Stilton.

(Continued on next page)

LONDON BURGER

(Continued)

Cook eggs: Use a paper towel to wipe excess fats out the frying pan. Return the pan to its burner. Over medium heat, melt 2 tablespoons of butter. Once butter has melted, crack the eggs into the pan, taking care to crack each egg on an opposite side of the pan. Keep the eggs separate as they cook. Cover the pan with a lid. Cook the eggs for 2 minutes. Whites should be opaque and fully cooked. Yolks should still be liquid. Use a spatula to remove each egg from the pan. Place an egg atop each hamburger patty.

Toast buns: Again, use a paper towel to wipe out residue from the pan. Return it to its burner and melt the remaining butter over medium heat. Once the butter is melted, place both buns, cut-side down, in the butter. Toast buns for 1–2 minutes. Remove when golden brown.

Assemble burgers: Place the bottom halves of the buns on plates. Use a fork to remove shallots from the oil. Place the shallots onto the buns, and gently flatten. Shallots should be soft enough to spread almost like butter. Add one slice of tomato to each bun, then place a patty (with its cheese and egg) onto each tomato. Spread the English mustard onto the toasted portion of the top bun. Place the top bun on the burger. Serve.

Makes 2 burgers

NYC BURGER

When Rory tags along with a group of new acquaintances to grab some burgers and drinks, they all head to P. J. Clarke's on Third Avenue in Midtown Manhattan. Since 1884 it's been a favorite spot for everyone from famous writers, to tourists, to Bloomingdale's execs.

Next time you are in NYC, stop at P. J. Clarke's for a burger. Until then, these burgers will help you recreate their casually sophisticated vibe right at home.

Ingredients:

1 batch béarnaise sauce

1 lb ground beef, Kobe preferred

2 t kosher salt

1 t black pepper

1 T butter

4–6 slices bacon, double-smoked preferred, cooked

Dill pickle spears, for serving, *optional*

2 brioche buns

Béarnaise Sauce

3 T white wine vinegar

1 T peeled and minced shallot

2 t minced fresh tarragon leaves

2 egg yolks

2 t water

¾ c butter

Kosher salt, to taste

Black pepper, to taste

Prepare béarnaise sauce: Combine vinegar, shallot, and tarragon leaves in a small saucepan. Over medium heat, bring to a boil, then promptly remove from heat. Combine egg yolks and water in blender. Blend on medium-low speed and spoon in 1 tablespoon of the vinegar mixture. Continue to drizzle in the remaining vinegar mixture in a thin, steady stream. Reduce blender speed to low. Place butter in saucepan and melt over medium heat. Once melted, turn blender up to medium-low speed and spoon in 1 tablespoon of butter. Drizzle in the remaining melted butter in a thin, steady stream. Continue to blend for 30 seconds. Remove sauce from blender. Stir in salt and pepper as desired. This is your béarnaise sauce.

Prepare hamburger patties: Separate ground beef into two 8-ounce balls. Roll each ball by hand, then flatten each to ½-inch thickness. Cup a patty from both sides with hands and gently press in to make it round, with no cracks around the edge. Repeat for each patty. Sprinkle ½ teaspoon of kosher salt and ¼ teaspoon of black pepper onto each side of each patty. Gently press salt and pepper into each patty before turning it over.

Cook hamburgers: Heat a large frying pan over high heat. Once the pan is hot, add the patties, leaving a little space between them. Cook the patties on one side for 3 minutes. Using a spatula, flip each patty. Cook the other side of the patties for 2 minutes more. Use the spatula to remove the patties from the pan, and place them on a plate, clean cutting board, or wire rack.

(Continued on next page)

NYC
BURGER

(Continued)

Toast the buns: Pour off excess grease from pan into a bowl or jar for disposal later. Add butter to pan and melt over medium heat. Place buns, cut-side down, in pan to sop up the melted butter and to toast. Once the buns turn a golden color on the toasted side, remove from pan. Place each bun on a separate plate.

Assemble burgers: Top each bottom bun with one cooked patty. Arrange bacon on patty, then spoon béarnaise sauce onto bacon. Place top bun atop the burger. Repeat for remaining patty. Garnish with pickles, if using. Serve.

Makes 2 half-pound burgers

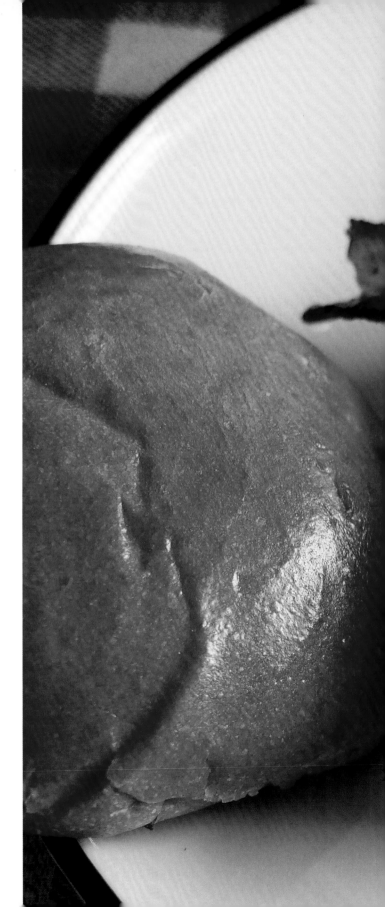

BURGER DAY

Since 2000 Luke and Lorelai have evolved from friendship to an on-again, off-again romance to full-blown partners. Now they are living together and sometimes working together.

Lorelai views herself and Luke as closely bonded, but are they? Emily calls them roommates.

They each manage their individual finances. They keep their businesses separate. They avoid telling each other important things, like Luke looking at potential locations to franchise the diner and Lorelai continuing to go to therapy without Emily.

Are they a solid couple, as good as married? Or is Emily right?

One thing is clear—Luke still loves Lorelai and will do anything to support her.

He has stepped up, once again, to help out at the Dragonfly by making lunch once a week on Burger Day. For Lorelai's guests, Luke would want to make this burger unique and memorable; therefore, this recipe is the Luke's Diner Cheeseburger reimagined, using homemade condiments and adding high-quality bacon.

Lunch at the Dragonfly is back, big time! One day a week.

Ingredients:

1 batch tomato jam, for serving

1 batch Dijon aioli, for serving

2 lb ground sirloin

3 t kosher salt

1½ t black pepper

6 slices Wisconsin cheddar cheese

6 fresh and soft sesame-seed buns

12 strips applewood-smoked bacon, cooked, for serving

1 c dill pickle chips, for serving

6 leaves iceberg lettuce, for serving

6 thin slices red onion, for serving

Tomato Jam

2 lb Roma, cherry, or grape tomatoes, finely chopped

½ c sugar

2 T brown sugar

1 T lime juice

¾ t citric acid

1 T apple cider vinegar

¼ c minced red onion

1 T peeled and minced fresh ginger

1 T crushed red pepper flakes

½ t kosher salt

½ t cinnamon

⅛ t ground cloves

1 t balsamic vinegar

Dijon Aioli

1 large egg yolk

2 t freshly squeezed lemon juice

¼ t grated lemon zest

¼ t kosher salt

1 c olive oil

2 t Dijon mustard

(Continued on next page)

BURGER DAY

(Continued)

Make jam: Combine all ingredients except balsamic vinegar in a large saucepan. Over medium-high heat, stir to combine. Bring to a boil, then reduce heat. Allow the mixture to simmer for 1 hour, stirring occasionally. At the one-hour mark, stir in the balsamic vinegar. Simmer for 15 minutes more. Once jam has thickened, remove from heat. Allow to cool fully before refrigerating.

Mix aioli: In a large bowl, using an electric mixer on medium-low speed, combine egg yolk, lemon juice, lemon zest, and salt. While continuing to beat the mixture, add a small drop of olive oil. Once it is fully incorporated, add 2 drops of olive oil. Slowly increase the amount of olive oil added, making sure to fully beat in each addition before adding more. Once the full cup of olive oil has been added, the mixture should be fluffy and creamy. Stir in Dijon mustard and mix until incorporated. Set aside.

Prepare hamburger patties: Separate ground sirloin into six equal balls. Roll each ball by hand, then flatten each to ½-inch thickness. Cup a patty from both sides with hands and gently press in to make it round, with no cracks around the edge. Repeat for each patty. Sprinkle ½ teaspoon of kosher salt and ¼ teaspoon of black pepper onto each side of each patty. Gently press salt and pepper into each patty before turning it over.

Cook hamburgers: Heat a large frying pan over high heat. Once the pan is hot, add three patties, leaving a little space between them. Cook the patties on one side for 3 minutes. Using a spatula, flip each patty. Cook the other side of the patties for 2 minutes more. Add 1 slice of cheddar cheese to each patty during the final minute of cooking. Use the spatula to remove the patties from the pan, and place them on a plate, clean cutting board, or wire rack. Tent the burgers with aluminum foil so they stay warm. Use a paper towel to wipe out the fat from the pan, into the trash bin. Repeat this process for the remaining 3 patties.

Assemble burgers: Place a patty inside one sesame seed bun. Spread tomato jam and Dijon aioli on underside of top bun. Top patty with bacon, pickles, lettuce, and onion. Place top bun on the burger. Repeat for remaining patties. Serve.

Makes 6 burgers

POUTINE

Surrounded by so many foods of the world at the International Food Festival, what does Lorelai choose to eat first?

She wanders over to the annual basket-bidding event and bids on some poor young woman's basket. Luke tries to tell her that Cassie wants a guy to bid on her basket, not some nutty, overly caffeinated older woman. Lorelai won't relent. She wins the basket.

Instead of sampling her way around the square, touring the world through food, she eats her way through a very awkward picnic with Cassie. No poutine. No Swedish meatballs. Not even any sangria! Nothing. Well, she always has next year.

You don't have to wait until next year! Enjoy this quick poutine at home. You'll be taking up curling in no time.

Ingredients:

1 T butter

½ c peeled, minced shallots

2 cloves garlic, peeled and minced

Black pepper

¼ c butter

¼ c flour

2½ c beef broth

1½ c chicken broth

1 T Worcestershire sauce

1 t beef base or 1 cube beef bouillon

1 T sherry

3 T minced fresh parsley

1 batch French fries, cooked, from frozen or using the Basket of Fries recipe (page 79)

5–6 oz cheese curds (may substitute grated mozzarella)

Sauté shallot: In a Dutch oven or large saucepan, melt 1 tablespoon of butter. Sauté shallots and garlic. Add black pepper. Remove from pan and set aside.

Make gravy: In the same pan, melt ¼ cup butter. Add flour and stir to combine until a smooth paste forms. Add broths, Worcestershire sauce, soup base or bouillon, and sherry. Stir to combine. Bring to a boil. Reduce heat. Stir in the shallot and garlic mixture. Simmer until reduced and thickened. Add parsley.

Assemble poutine: On a large plate or low rimmed bowl, arrange French fries. Spoon gravy over the fries. Top with cheese curds. Serve.

Makes 3–4 servings

SPRING

BASKET OF FRIES

At least when Rory is flitting around London, lunching at the club with Naomi, drinking bottles of wine with Logan that cost as much as a car payment, she's also staying true to her Lorelai-instilled roots.

How do we know?

At her fancy, suits-and-skirts lunch with Logan, she orders a basket of fries with her meal. It's a nod to Stars Hollow, in the middle of Huntzberger World.

Ingredients:

2 lb russet potatoes (weigh after peeling & removing dark spots)

2 c water

⅓ c sugar

32 oz high-oleic sunflower or vegetable oil

Salt, *optional*

Makes 80–100 fries

Cut potatoes: Using a sharp knife, cut each russet potato into slices ¼- to ½-inch thick. Cut each slice into ¼- to ½-inch wide potato strips. These are your fries!

Soak fries: In a large ziplock bag, combine fries, water, and sugar. Seal the bag. Fill the sink or a large bowl with ice. Place the bag into the ice. After 30 minutes, drain out the water and pat the potatoes dry.

Set up a draining rack: Cover a plate, cutting board, or countertop with a double layer of paper towels. Place a wire rack on top of the paper towels. Reserve for use later.

Fry potatoes: In a deep-fryer or a Dutch oven, heat oil to 300°F. Working in batches, deep-fry potatoes in oil for 4 minutes. Remove potatoes using the deep-frying basket, a slotted spoon, or similar. Place potatoes on the draining rack.

Fry potatoes again: Once all potatoes have been deep-fried, increase the oil heat to 375°F. Working in batches, deep-fry the potatoes again. This time leave them in the oil until they reach the desired color and doneness, roughly 5–7 minutes. Once done, remove using the deep-frying basket, a slotted spoon, or similar. Place fries on the draining rack.

Serve: Salt the fries, if using.

SALCHIPAPAS

FESTIVAL FOOD

Taylor is still town selectman. He's still presiding over the town meetings, coming up with new ideas for town festivals and events to raise money for improvements, and terrorizing Luke.

This time the topic is a new sewer system. Taylor wants Luke to write a testimonial to help get the town's plumbing updated. Sticking to their time-tested tradition, Luke refuses. He continues to refuse each time Taylor hounds him.

One day in the diner, after a round of verbal sparring with Luke, Taylor cracks. He has a mini-meltdown and yells out to all of Luke's customers that the Wi-Fi password is fake.

When Taylor tells everyone that the diner isn't their office and they all need to go home, Luke gives in and takes the clipboard to write his testimonial.

What was it that tipped the scales for Luke? Was it Taylor's defense of his "no Wi-Fi" policy? Or did Luke feel bad for pushing Taylor to the brink?

Regardless, it's nice to see the ebb and flow of their relationship play out again, just like old times.

Ingredients:

1 (28-oz) bag frozen steak fries

6–8 uncured all-beef hot dogs

1–2 T high-oleic sunflower or vegetable oil

¼ c mayonnaise

3 T Peruvian aji chili paste

Mustard, for serving

Ketchup, for servings

Makes 3–4 servings

Bake steak fries: Follow instructions on bag to cook fries in oven.

Cook hot dogs: Place the hot dogs in a saucepan and cover with water. Over medium-high heat, bring water to a simmer. Simmer hot dogs for 5 minutes. Remove from heat and drain water. Cut hot dogs into diagonal slices, roughly one half-inch thick. In a frying pan, heat the oil over medium-high heat. Once oil is hot, add hot dog slices. Flip hot dog slices often, cooking for 5–6 minutes until edges begin to brown. Remove from heat.

Assemble: Arrange steak fries on a platter. Top with hot dog slices. Lightly toss to combine.

Make aji sauce: In a small bowl, combine mayonnaise and aji paste. Stir to mix thoroughly.

Serve: Portion out the steak fries and hot dog slices into 6 servings. Serve with small dipping bowls of aji sauce, mustard, and ketchup.

HOT DOG CART

NEW YORK

Throughout the original seven seasons, hot dogs are not mentioned often. The most memorable hot dog moment occurs when Kirk dresses up as one and stands in front of the diner, advertising lunch at the Dragonfly.

However, in the revival, hot dogs, and more specifically, the hot dog cart, have been elevated to star status after making three appearances. Rory buys Paris's children dinner at the hot dog cart in the local park. Lorelai smooth-talks the man running a New York City cart and scores some hot dogs at 7 a.m. Finally, Lorelai tells Rory she and Luke are having a hot dog cart at the wedding reception. The guests won't have to pay. It will be "open cart." After all, she's a Gilmore.

Ingredients:

8 all-beef hot dogs

8 hot dog buns

12 oz mustard, for serving

12 oz ketchup, for serving

1 c diced onion, for serving

1 (10-oz) jar dill or sweet relish, for serving

1 batch coleslaw (page 84), for serving

1 batch hot dog chili (page 84), for serving

1 batch red sauce (page 85), for serving

Boil hot dogs: Place hot dogs in a large saucepan. Cover with water. Over medium-high heat, bring water to a boil. Reduce heat to low. Simmer hot dogs for 12 minutes.

Steam buns: While hot dogs are simmering, place a wire rack over the saucepan. Place buns on the rack, two at a time. Allow steam from hot dogs to warm and moisten the buns. Once buns feel soft and warm, remove. Wrap buns in aluminum foil to retain heat and moisture. Repeat until all buns have been steamed.

Assemble and serve: Use tongs or a fork to remove a hot dog from the water. Place hot dog in a steamed bun. Repeat for remaining hot dogs. Add toppings as desired. Serve.

Makes 4–8 servings

(Continued on next page)

SPRING

HOT DOG CART (Continued)

HOT DOG CHILI

Ingredients:

½ lb ground beef

½ c chopped white onion

2 T chili powder

1 T cumin

2 T tomato paste

2 c water

1 T freshly squeezed lemon juice

1–2 t salt, to taste

1–2 T masa harina, to thicken

Brown meat: In a large saucepan or a deep frying pan, cook ground beef over medium-high heat. Use a wooden spoon to turn meat often. When beef is just beginning to turn brown, add onion. Continue to cook until beef has browned and onion is translucent.

Make chili: Add chili powder, cumin, and tomato paste to beef. Pour in water and lemon juice. Stir to combine until tomato paste has been fully incorporated into sauce. Bring to a boil. Reduce heat to medium-low and simmer for 20 minutes.

Season and thicken chili: Add salt, to taste. If a thicker consistency is desired, stir in masa harina in small increments, waiting 1–2 minutes between each addition, until chili reaches the desired consistency. Remove from heat. Serve.

COLESLAW

Ingredients:

3 c cabbage, finely sliced

1 small carrot, peeled, grated

Combine vegetables: In a medium bowl, combine cabbage and carrot. Set aside.

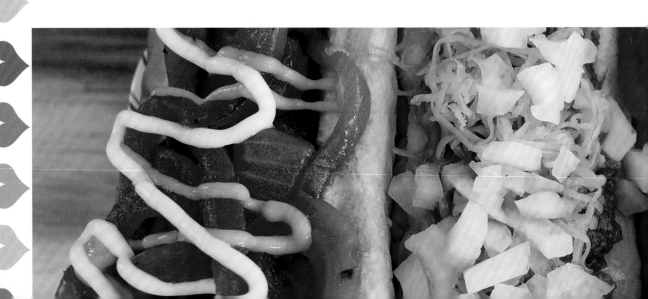

COLESLAW   (Continued)

½ c mayonnaise

1 T sugar

1 T grated onion with its liquid

1 t freshly squeezed lemon juice

1 t red wine vinegar

½ t Dijon mustard

½ t salt

½ t black pepper

Mix dressing: In a small bowl, combine mayonnaise, sugar, onion, lemon juice, vinegar, mustard, salt, and pepper. Stir to combine.

Make coleslaw: Stir dressing into vegetables until fully combined. Cover and refrigerate until needed.

RED SAUCE

Ingredients:

1 T olive oil

2 sweet yellow onions, sliced thin

6 T tomato paste

¼ c red wine vinegar

2–3 T Worcestershire sauce

2 T agave nectar or light corn syrup

1–2 T crushed red pepper flakes

3 c warm water

Sauté onions: In a large frying pan, heat oil over medium-high heat. Add onions, separating slices into rings. Continue to sauté until rings are soft and translucent.

Make sauce: In a medium bowl, combine tomato paste, vinegar, Worcestershire sauce, agave, crushed red pepper flakes, and warm water. Stir to combine until tomato paste has fully dissolved. Pour sauce into onions. Bring to a boil. Reduce heat to medium-low. Simmer for 20–30 minutes. Serve.

MAIN
DISHES

PARMESAN CUTLETS

Parmesan Cutlets is the final recipe from the Welcome Home dinner Luke prepares for Rory.

Two main courses, a salad, and garlic bread for three people? We are talking about Lorelai and Rory, but still.

No, wait. There's a fourth plate set. Who are we expecting?

Oh, yes. Paul! Kind, sweet, thoughtful Paul is coming to dinner.

Okay, forget about Paul. Everyone does. Just focus on serving up these cutlets. They're the next best thing to fried chicken!

Ingredients:

1 lb skinless chicken breast fillets

1 c flour

2 T Italian seasoning

1 T kosher salt

1 T black pepper

1 egg

⅓ c water

1 c bread crumbs

½ c Parmesan cheese

3 T olive oil

Prepare chicken: If the chicken breasts are especially thick, consider splitting each one by slicing it, horizontally, into two equal pieces. Wrap each chicken breast in wax paper. Use the flat side of a kitchen mallet to pound the chicken to ¾-inch thickness. Set aside.

Prepare flour: In a low-sided bowl, add flour, Italian seasoning, kosher salt, and pepper. Use a fork to mix.

Prepare egg: In a separate low-sided bowl, add egg and water. Use a fork to break yolk and lightly beat mixture until it is combined.

Prepare bread crumbs: In a third low-sided bowl, add bread crumbs and Parmesan cheese. Use a fork to mix.

Dredge chicken: Dip the first chicken breast piece into the flour mixture, taking care to fully cover both sides with flour. Next, dip it into the egg, again making sure the full piece is covered. Hold the chicken over the bowl for a moment to permit the excess liquid to run off, then dip the chicken into the bread crumbs and pat down until meat is fully breaded. Place breaded chicken on a plate. Repeat for each piece of chicken.

(Continued on next page)

PARMESAN CUTLETS

(Continued)

Set up a draining rack: Cover a plate, cutting board, or countertop with a double layer of paper towels. Place a wire rack on top of the paper towels. Reserve for use later.

Fry chicken: Heat a large saucepan over medium-high heat for 1–2 minutes. Add the olive oil. Wait 1–2 minutes more. When oil is hot, place the chicken pieces in the pan. Positioning them close together is fine. Cook for 2–3 minutes. Once the cooked side reaches a deep, golden brown, flip each piece using tongs, a spatula or a fork. Cook the second side for another 2–3 minutes. Remove chicken from pan and place on wire rack. Allow to rest for 5 minutes. Serve.

Makes 4 servings

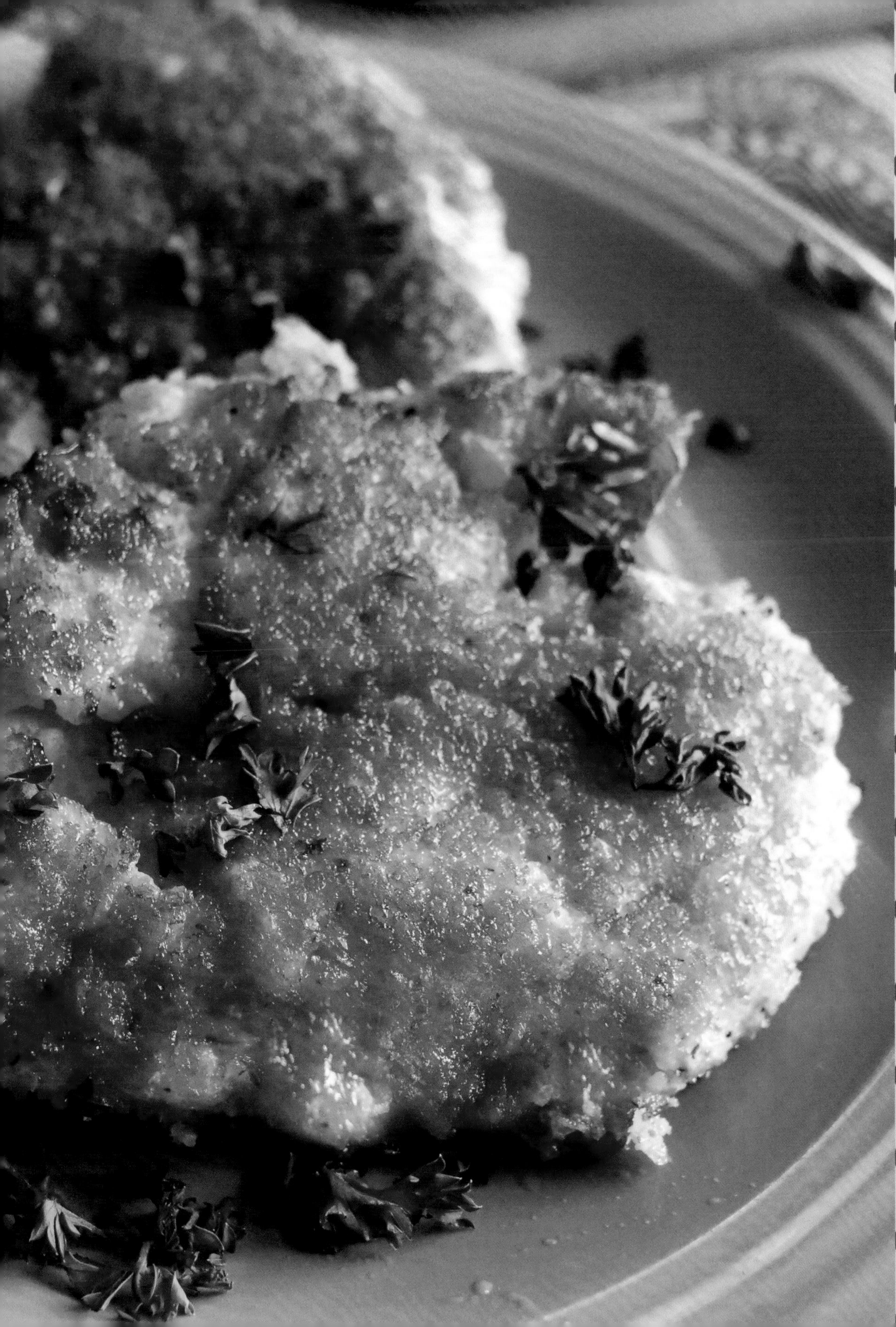

LOBSTER MAC 'N' CHEESE

Remember when Luke tried the lobster Logan made and loved it so much he told Lorelai he wanted to serve lobster at their wedding?

Time has passed, of course, and Lorelai did mention the hot dog cart for their wedding. Do they serve lobster, as well?

While we have no way of knowing what foods he and Lorelai did serve on the big day, the macaroni and cheese Luke makes for both Rory's welcome home and for April's visit does appear to have chunks of lobster in it. It may not be Martha's Vineyard, but adding lobster to a dish at home still adds rich flavor and a feeling of decadence!

This recipe is designed to make a main dish. It also works perfectly well in the Gilmore fashion, as a side dish. If it is Movie Night, have it as an appetizer. No nose ring required!

Ingredients:

2 T + 1 t salt, divided, plus more to taste

2 lb thawed and rinsed uncooked lobster tails

½ lb cavatappi or elbow macaroni

1 T olive oil

½ c butter

2 T flour

1 c heavy cream

1 c milk (may substitute 2 cups half-and-half for heavy cream and milk)

2 c grated Havarti

1 c grated Gruyère

¼ t white pepper

¼ t cayenne pepper

⅓ c panko bread crumbs

2–3 T t chopped fresh thyme leaves

Cook lobster tails: Fill a Dutch oven or small stockpot halfway with water. Over high heat, bring water to a boil. Add 2 tablespoons of salt to water. Carefully place each lobster tail in the water. Cook until the flesh is a pinkish white and the shell is red. Use tongs or a slotted spoon to remove from water.

Prepare lobster tails: Once the lobster shells have cooled to the touch, use kitchen scissors to cut the shell down the middle, from open end to tail. Pry open the shell and remove the meat. Look for a dark line along the underside of the meat. Remove this vein, then rinse the meat and pat dry. Cut the lobster meat into 1-inch cubes. Set aside.

Cook pasta: Boil water in a large saucepan or Dutch oven. Add 1 teaspoon of salt. Add pasta. Stir to prevent pasta from clumping. Cook for the minimum amount of time noted on the package, or even 1 minute less. When pasta is al dente, or even a bit harder, remove from heat and strain. Toss with 1 tablespoon of olive oil to prevent clumping. Set aside.

(Continued on next page)

LOBSTER MAC 'N' CHEESE

(Continued)

Preheat oven: Ensure oven rack is positioned in the center of oven. Preheat oven to 350°F.

Make cheese sauce: In a medium saucepan, melt butter over medium-high heat. Stir flour into butter until it forms a paste. Add heavy cream and milk and stir to remove lumps. Add cheeses, white pepper, and cayenne. This is your cheese sauce!

Bake pasta: In a medium baking dish or gratin, add arrange pasta in a level layer. Pour cheese sauce over the top. Fold in lobster pieces. Top with panko. Place in oven and bake for 20 minutes. Remove from oven, top with thyme leaves, and let cool. Serve.

Makes 3–4 servings as a main

Makes 6–8 servings as a side

CONTRIBUTED BY
ROSE ABDOO

SWEET POTATO PEANUT STEW

"I love peanut butter and never have it in the house because when I lived alone, I realized I would eat the creamy kind so fast and always wanted to blame others for the empty jar. Alas, I came to the slow-dawning realization that it was all me! Nowadays, I don't allow myself peanut butter in the home. But! If I visit you and you have some in your pantry, I would like to make this stew together! Peanut butter dreams, my friend!!"

—Rose Abdoo, "Gypsy" and "Berta" in *Gilmore Girls: A Year in the Life*

Ingredients:

4 c peeled and diced sweet potatoes

1 red onion, peeled, thinly sliced, quartered

1½ c chopped broccoli

1½ c chopped cauliflower

⅓ c seeded and chopped red bell pepper

1 (14.5-oz) can diced tomatoes

4 sprigs flat-leaf parsley

1 T curry powder

1 t kosher salt

½ t ground allspice

½ t black pepper

2 c water

½ c creamy peanut butter

½ c chopped flat-leaf parsley

Combine ingredients in cooker: Stir together all ingredients (except set aside peanut butter and ½ cup chopped parsley for later) in a slow cooker or multi-cooker until thoroughly combined.

Cook: Cover and cook for 90 minutes on high. Stir in peanut butter. Cover and continue to cook for 30 minutes.

Serve: Just before serving, discard parsley sprigs. Stir in chopped parsley.

Makes 6 servings

Rose Abdoo is known for her role as "Gypsy" in Gilmore Girls. *In* Gilmore Girls: A Year in the Life *she plays both "Gypsy" and "Berta." Rose's 2021 roles include "Ms. Mandrake" in the new* Saved by the Bell *on Peacock and "Josefina" in* Hacks *on HBO/Max. Rose also voices several characters in* Madagascar: A Little Wild. *Connect with Rose on Instagram: @roseabdoo*

CHICKEN SCALOPPINE

TOWN FAVORITE

When we see Luke and Lorelai relax on the sofa with some Italian takeout and a bottle of wine, it's clear Lorelai has upped her game. This isn't her standard takeout order involving pizza boxes and Chinese food containers; it's actual meals. Paul Anka, the dog, even gets his own hanger steak.

While they eat, Lorelai voices her concerns about Michel leaving the inn, telling Luke that Michel thinks the inn needs to expand, to grow. Luke hears the word "grow" and freaks out. He shuts her down just like he did when she wanted to meet with Mike Armstrong to discuss the possibility of selling the inn. What is with him?

Later that night, Lorelai dreams about the real Paul Anka for the third time in six months. She wakes up, goes down to make some coffee, and calls Rory in London to tell her about Michel. Rory listens. Rory reassures her. Why couldn't Luke have done the same?

Chicken Scaloppine is the dish Luke ordered from the mysterious new restaurant in town. He may not be the best listener, but he sure does choose tasty meals!

Ingredients:

½ c flour

2 t kosher salt

1 t black pepper

½ t crushed red pepper flakes

1 lb chicken breast fillets, sliced or pounded to ¼-inch thickness

¼ c olive oil

½ yellow or white onion, thinly sliced

½ lb cremini mushrooms, sliced

¼ c sherry

1 T butter

¼ c chopped flat-leaf parsley leaves, chopped

Makes 2–4 servings

Prepare flour: In a low-sided bowl, combine flour, kosher salt, black pepper, and crushed red pepper flakes. Use a fork to mix.

Dredge chicken: Dip the first chicken breast piece into the flour mixture, taking care to fully cover both sides with flour. Place floured chicken on a plate. Repeat for each piece of chicken.

Cook onions and mushrooms: Heat a large saucepan over medium-high heat for 1–2 minutes. Add 2 tablespoons of olive oil. Wait 1–2 minutes more. When oil is hot, separate onion slices into rings as they are added to the pan. Add mushrooms. Sauté vegetables until onions are translucent and mushrooms are tender. Use a slotted spoon to remove vegetables from pan. Place them in a bowl. Set aside.

Cook chicken: Increase heat to high. Add the remaining olive oil. When oil is hot, place the chicken pieces in the pan. Positioning them close together is fine. Cook for 1–2 minutes on each side. Remove chicken to a plate.

Make scaloppine: Reduce heat to low. Deglaze pan by adding the sherry and using an inverted spatula to scrape the bottom of the pan. Add butter. As butter melts, stir to combine with sherry. Reduce heat to a simmer. Add chicken and vegetables back into the pan. Sprinkle with parsley. Simmer for 5–7 minutes. Remove from heat. Allow to rest for 5 minutes. Serve.

LINGUINE & MEATBALLS

TOWN FAVORITE

Lorelai orders linguine and meatballs for herself, which is an odd combination. Spaghetti and meatballs is the traditional dish.

Has she changed to linguine because spaghetti makes her and Rory aggressive? Does the sauce-to-noodle ratio improve with linguine?

Lorelai never says why she chose linguine. Maybe you can figure it out at home.

This recipe takes some time, but it's pretty simple to make, and your home will smell magnificent!

Ingredients:

Sauce

2 T olive oil

1 c chopped yellow or white onion

2–3 cloves garlic, peeled, smashed

¾ c peeled and chopped carrot

¾ c topped and chopped celery

1 T kosher salt, *divided*

Black pepper, to taste

2 (28-oz) cans tomatoes, whole, peeled, preferably imported from Italy

28 ounces water

1 c merlot or similar dry red wine

3 T freshly squeezed lemon juice

3 T butter

½ c chopped flat-leaf parsley

½ c chopped fresh basil

1 lb uncooked linguine

Meatballs

½ lb ground beef

½ lb hot or sweet Italian sausage

⅓ c finely chopped yellow or white onion

3 cloves garlic, peeled and minced

¼ c fresh parsley

½ c plain bread crumbs

½ c grated Parmesan cheese

1 t kosher salt

1 t dried oregano

1 t dried basil

½ t black pepper

1 egg

Sauté vegetables: Heat oil in Dutch oven or 6-quart pot over medium-high heat. Add onion, garlic, carrot, and celery. Sauté vegetables, stirring often, until onions are translucent; about 12 minutes. Sprinkle vegetables with 1 teaspoon of kosher salt and a few pinches of black pepper.

(Continued on next page)

SPRING

LINGUINE & MEATBALLS

(Continued)

Make sauce: Add canned tomatoes, water and wine to pot. Stir to combine. Bring to a boil, then reduce heat to medium-low. Simmer for 30 minutes, stirring periodically.

Prepare meatballs: Place ground beef in a large bowl. Remove any casings from Italian sausage and add to bowl. Add onion, garlic, parsley, bread crumbs, Parmesan cheese, salt, oregano, basil, black pepper, and egg to the bowl. Wearing gloves, work the ingredients together until they are all combined and evenly distributed.

Roll meatballs: Separate meat mixture into eight 3-ounce portions. Roll each portion into a 2-inch ball. Set aside.

Blend sauce: Working in batches, transfer sauce to blender, filling blender 50– 60 percent full. Blend each batch until it is free of chunks, then pour sauce into a large bowl or pot before repeating with the next batch. Once all sauce has been blended, return it to the original pot, over medium-low heat. Stir in lemon juice, butter, fresh herbs, and the remaining 2 teaspoons of salt. If making meatballs, add them to sauce now. Simmer for 20 minutes, uncovered, untouched.

Simmer sauce: After 20 minutes, gently stir sauce with meatballs. Continue simmering for 1 hour, stirring occasionally.

Cook linguine: Prepare linguine according to instructions on box.

Serve: On a plate or in a pasta bowl, add linguine. Add sauce and two meatballs. Serve with extra Parmesan cheese.

Makes 4 servings

SWEDISH MEATBALLS

Very briefly, we catch a glimpse of Jackson at the International Food Festival. He and Sookie are still together, but their living arrangements are unclear, especially considering Lane, Zack, and their two sons have moved into the Bellevilles' old house.

He seems chipper, though, standing beside the booth showcasing all of his beautifully grown vegetables. At least that part hasn't changed!

Pair up this dish with some fresh steamed veggies of your own. Don't let the long list of ingredients fool you. This recipe is pretty simple to make, even for a weeknight dinner. Plus, once you've tried these meatballs, you won't be able to live without them, just like Jackson can't live without Sookie.

Ingredients:

Meatballs

1 lb ground beef

½ lb ground pork

½ c grated white onion with its liquid

⅓ c bread crumbs

2 T evaporated milk

¼ c finely chopped parsley

1 clove garlic, peeled and minced

1 t kosher salt

¼ t black pepper

⅛ t white pepper

¼ t ground allspice

⅛ t ground nutmeg

1 egg

3 T butter

Sauce

2 T sherry

5 T butter

⅓ c flour

2 c chicken broth

2 c beef broth

1 c heavy cream

2 T Worcestershire sauce

¾ t Dijon mustard

1 t salt

½ t black pepper

Finely chopped parsley, for serving

Prepare meatballs: In a large bowl, combine ground beef, ground pork, onion, bread crumbs, milk, parsley, garlic, kosher salt, peppers, spices, and egg. Use hands, covered by latex or nitrile gloves, mix the ingredients together, until fully incorporated and evenly distributed. Divide into 25 portions. Roll each portion into a ball.

(Continued on next page)

SWEDISH MEATBALLS

(Continued)

Brown meatballs: In a large, deep frying pan, melt butter over medium-high heat. Add meatballs. If all do not fit, work in batches. Allow meatballs to cook for 2–3 minutes, then flip them to cook an additional 2 minutes on the other side. Once balls are fully browned on all sides, use tongs to remove each from pan and place into a bowl. Set aside.

Make sauce: With burner still set to medium-high, drain excess grease into a small container. Return pan to burner and use sherry to deglaze bottom of pan. Add butter. Once butter is melted, add flour. Stir butter and flour together using wooden spoon until a loose paste forms. Add both broths, heavy cream, Worcestershire sauce, mustard, salt, and pepper. Stir to combine. Bring to a boil.

Simmer sauce and meatballs: Once sauce boils, reduce heat to a simmer. Simmer for 10 minutes, stirring occasionally. Gently add meatballs back to the pan. Simmer for 10 minutes more.

Serve: Spoon the sauce and meatballs over a bed of mashed potatoes or egg noodles. Garnish with chopped parsley. Serve.

Makes 5–6 servings

CONTRIBUTED BY
TODD LOWE

MIGAS

CAST & CREW

"What is Migas? It's a skillet brunch for a football Sunday. Not terribly healthy, but eco-friendly. The bacon grease gets reused to sauté all those onions, peppers, and flour tortillas. The tortillas become chips.

Go favorite team on Sunday!".

—Todd Lowe, "Zack" in *Gilmore Girls: A Year in the Life*

Ingredients:

1 package bacon

8 flour (YES) or corn (MEH) tortillas, cut or torn into chip-size triangles

2 or 3 cloves garlic, sliced thin

1 onion, chopped

5 bell peppers (of different colors-Zesty!), seeded and sliced into long strips

Dash cumin

Dash salt

Dash pepper

½ stick butter

12 eggs, lightly beaten

1 or 2 tomatoes, diced (helps if they're a tad frozen for firmness)

Handful or 2 of shredded cheese (cheddar Jack melts well)

Jalapeño peppers, sliced, *optional*

Hot sauce, *optional*

Salsa, *optional*

Cook a buttload of bacon in the largest skillet you have. Remove bacon, but don't drain that grease! The grease will be put to good use! (Okay, there may be some excess grease, but trust me, you'll want it to make your chips.)

Get the grease very hot hot hot! Be careful. It might splatter. Best to wear an apron.

Add half of your tortilla pieces to sop up the hot grease. Fry quickly to get them firm, crispy, and golden brown. Remove with tongs and set these chips aside with your bacon on a plate with some paper towels. There may be more grease than you want, so you can wad up a bunch of paper towels and sop it up and discard, or you can do like my Meemaw in Texas and pour it into an old coffee can for later use.

Bring the temperature down then add your garlic, onion, peppers and dashes of spices. Hey, a half stick of butter could be welcome here, as well. That's a lot of peppers. Sauté them for a minute or so and throw in your remaining tortilla pieces. The tortillas won't get as firm this time. Just make sure you stir them around the pan with the veggies.

After a couple more minutes, push all that to the side of the pan and pour in your lightly beaten eggs. Let them cackleberries fill the pan and scramble. Gradually start folding the tortillas and peppers in with the eggs.

(Continued on next page)

MIGAS

(Continued)

Finally, add your tomaters. They're coming in last so they shouldn't get too mushy. Give another stir and fold or two and admire your Technicolor brunch, but don't share the pic on the socials just yet. Cover with cheese and garnish the side of the skillet with your homemade chips! Now take that photo.

You can play around with sliced jalapeños on the side, but probably best not to cook with them as not everyone can take the heat. Hot sauce/salsa can be a necessary application as well.

You can feed 4–7 hungry peeps

Todd Lowe is an actor who played "Zack van Gerbig" in Gilmore Girls and Gilmore Girls: A Year in the Life. His other roles include "Terry Bellafleur" in True Blood, and "Eric" in The Princess Diaries, among many others.

In addition to his roles in television, film, and stage plays, Todd is also a singer/songwriter and musician who often plays with his band, The LA Hootenanny, in and around Los Angeles, where he resides.

BEEF BULGOGI

Lane and Mrs. Kim have a booth at the International Food Festival, serving traditional Korean foods with a surprising twist. It seems like they are serving meat at the booth. This doesn't seem to be a one-time deal, either. Mrs. Kim admits to feeding eggs to the members of her new band.

What happened to the eggless egg salad?

Oh, and we finally get to see the ever-absent Mister Kim! Did his return put an end to her meatless days?

You don't have to put an end to your meatless days. This recipe works with a variety of ingredients other than steak. Try it with mushrooms, tofu, or a vegan meat substitute!

Ingredients:

2 lb boneless ribeye steak, excess fat removed

2 T soy sauce

2 T Korean chili paste/gochujang (may substitute sambal)

½ pear, grated

1 T peeled and grated fresh ginger

2 cloves garlic, peeled and minced

1 T packed light or dark brown sugar

1 T sesame oil

⅓ c high-oleic sunflower or vegetable oil

Cooked white or brown rice, for serving

Green onions, for serving

Sesame seeds, for serving

Prepare meat: Slice beef into ¼-inch strips, across the grain. Set aside.

Marinate meat: In a medium bowl or pan or a large ziplock bag, combine soy sauce, chili paste, pear, ginger, garlic, brown sugar, and sesame oil. Add meat slices. Cover bowl/ pan or seal the bag. Refrigerate for 4–6 hours.

Cook meat: Heat a large frying pan or cast-iron skillet over high heat. Add 2 tablespoons oil. Drain marinade from meat. Once oil is very hot, add a quarter of the meat to the pan. Cook it in a single layer, turning pieces often to ensure even cooking. When beef is fully cooked, use tongs or a slotted spoon to remove pieces to a plate. Repeat process for remainder of beef, adding oil as needed.

Serve: Serve with cooked rice. Garnish with green onions and sesame seeds.

Makes 4–6 servings

SHEPHERD'S PIE

When Rory's visit to London at the end of "Spring" gets cut short, she assumes it's because Logan's fiancée, Odette, is coming to town. What she doesn't know is—it's not a visit. Logan has failed to mention a critical piece of information. Odette is moving in with him.

Though they don't realize it, this is their final tryst in London.

Thinking this will be a typical "goodbye dinner," they mark Rory's departure in their usual fashion—by meeting at The Ivy.

The Ivy offers many signature dishes*, but this one was chosen to represent Rory. While it is decidedly British, it's also, technically, pie.

Ingredients:

1 T high-oleic sunflower or vegetable oil

⅓ c shallots

⅓ c peeled and diced carrots

⅓ c diced celery

1 c stemmed and finely chopped white mushrooms

¾ lb ground beef

¾ lb ground lamb

1 (14-oz) can whole tomatoes, roughly chopped

¼ c red wine

¼ c Worcestershire sauce

2 T dried thyme

¼ c flour

2 c beef broth

1–2 t kosher salt

1 t freshly cracked black pepper

Mint, fresh, chiffonade, as garnish

Mashed Potatoes

2 lb Yukon Gold potatoes, peeled and cubed

2 t sea salt

6 T butter

⅔ c milk or oat milk

2 c grated sharp cheddar cheese

1 t kosher salt

¾ t white pepper

Sauté vegetables: Heat oil in Dutch oven over medium-high heat. Once oil is hot, sauté shallots, carrots, celery, and mushrooms. Remove vegetables from pan into a bowl, using a slotted spoon. Set aside.

Brown meats: Return the pan to burner. Add ground beef and ground lamb. Over medium-high heat, brown meats. Strain, eliminating 95 percent of fats and juices.

Prepare the meat filling: Return meats to pan. Add sautéed vegetables. Add tomatoes, wine, Worcestershire sauce, and thyme. Over medium heat, reduce until meat appears moist but there is no pooling of liquid.

(Continued on next page)

SHEPHERD'S PIE

(Continued)

Thicken filling: Add flour. Gently incorporate it into the meat mixture until evenly dispersed and fully absorbed. Add broth. Stir. Season with salt and pepper, to taste. Simmer 30 minutes over medium-low heat.

Boil potatoes: Place potato cubes in a medium saucepan. Add enough water to cover potatoes. Add salt. Bring to a boil over medium-high heat. Reduce heat to medium, and continue to boil for 8–10 minutes. Test potatoes for doneness by poking a fork into a cube. As soon as the fork goes easily into the cube, remove from heat and drain water.

Prepare oven and pans: Ensure oven rack is in center position. Preheat oven to 400°F. Place 4 mini springform pans, one 8x8 inch square baking pan or an 8-inch pie plate onto a baking sheet. The baking sheet will catch any ingredients that may bubble over during baking. Set aside.

Mash potatoes: Add butter, milk, cheese, salt, and white pepper to potatoes. Use an electric hand mixer to combine ingredients and mash the potatoes. Continue to beat until potatoes have reached a smooth consistency. Assemble a piping bag with a large, open star tip. Spoon mashed potatoes into piping bag. Set aside.

Assemble pie(s): Spoon meat filling into pan(s). Pipe mashed potatoes onto the top in the desired pattern, making sure to cover the entire surface.

Bake pie(s): Place baking dish(es) and baking sheet in oven. Bake for 25–35 minutes. Once the tops of the potatoes have reached an even, golden-brown color, remove from oven. Let cool.

Serve: For springform pans, once pan is cool enough to touch, place pan onto serving dish, remove external ring, then use small tongs and a spatula to remove the pan's bottom, while simultaneously retaining the shape of the pie. If using one square or round pan, simply cut the pie into portions and use a large spoon to serve. Add mint to top as garnish. Serve.

Makes 4 servings

*This is not the actual recipe used by The Ivy.

SWEET
TREATS

BANANA FUDGE MILKSHAKE

Did you think we'd return to Stars Hollow to find Kirk had settled down with Lulu and, after all of his years of dabbling, finally decided on one career in which to throw all of his energy? Well, that's not quite how it went.

Yes, he has settled down with Lulu. The town even got them a pet pig to quash their talk of creating an actual human child. When it comes to his employment, though, Kirk is still dabbling.

His latest venture is a cumbersome, inefficient rideshare business. Lorelai tries to point out the holes in his idea, but he pooh-poohs her points and launches anyway.

As soon as Kirk drops off his first official customer, he bursts into the diner, visibly on a high. He celebrates by ordering this milkshake from Luke's.

His blip of success quickly turns into failure when the business gets shut down due to its unoriginal name. This result is not surprising to anyone but Kirk. Poor Kirk.

This milkshake works both ways—for celebrating and for wallowing. No matter the circumstances, it does the job, just like Kirk.

Ingredients:

¼–½ c fudge sauce (page 122)

1 c vanilla bean ice cream

1 large banana

¼ c milk

Whipped cream

1 maraschino cherry, for serving

1 chocolate bar, shaved, for serving

Prepare the glass: Using a spoon or food-safe brush, spread fudge sauce along the inside of the milkshake glass in a design of your choosing. Place the glass in the freezer for a few minutes.

Blend milkshake: In a blender, combine ice cream, banana, and milk. Blend until fully combined, and banana pieces have all been liquified.

Assemble: Pour milkshake into the chilled glass. Top with whipped cream and cherry. Sprinkle chocolate shavings around the top, if using. Serve.

Makes 1 milkshake

(Continued on next page)

BANANA FUDGE MILKSHAKE

(Continued)

Fudge Sauce

½ c evaporated milk

¼ c butter, cubed

4 oz unsweetened baking chocolate, chopped

1⅓ c sugar

1 t vanilla extract

Melt butter and chocolate: In a medium saucepan, heat milk over medium-high heat until bubbles appear around the edge. Remove from heat. Add butter and chocolate. Let stand 5 minutes, then stir until both butter and chocolate are fully melted and combined with milk.

Make sauce: Stir in sugar and vanilla. Return to medium-high heat and bring to a low boil. Reduce heat to medium. Continue to cook for 4 minutes or until thickened. Remove from heat. Let cool. Serve.

To store: Cool to room temperature. Cover and refrigerate.

BROWNIE BITES

Feeling inspired after a conversation with Jess, Rory decides to write a book based on her early life, growing up with Lorelai. When she tells Lorelai, Lorelai flips. At first, Rory is confused by her mother's reaction.

She shouldn't have been surprised. Had she thought about the book from Lorelai's perspective at all, she could have predicted the response.

Isn't Lorelai the woman who, at 17, bolted from her parents' home with her baby in tow to live in a shed and work as a maid, simply so she could achieve some level of independence and privacy? The townspeople know Lorelai, yes, but no one else does. She likes it that way. She's protective of Rory and of herself. Teenager or not, the second Lorelai gave birth, she became a mama bear.

When Rory confides in Lane about Lorelai's reaction, Lane responds by telling a story from years prior, when a woman called Rory illegitimate and Lorelai beaned the woman with brownie bites.

Lorelai has never wanted her life choices to be scrutinized by her parents, or their crowd, or anyone else. In Lorelai's way of thinking, a tell-all book was out of the question. It would, well, tell all . . . and open up both of them to scrutiny and judgment.

Fortunately for Rory, Lorelai didn't have any brownie bites to fling at her.

Ingredients:

1 c flour

½ t baking soda

¼ t salt

½ c softened butter

⅓ c cocoa powder

1 c sugar

1 egg, lightly beaten

2 T water

1 t vanilla extract

½ c semisweet chocolate chips

Makes 30 brownie bites

Prepare oven and pan: Ensure oven rack is positioned in center of oven. Set out a 12-cup mini tart or mini muffin pan. If pan coating is not nonstick, grease the inside of each cup using butter, shortening, or oil. Set aside.

Combine dry ingredients: In a small bowl, combine flour, baking soda, and salt. Lightly mix with a fork.

Cream butter: In a medium bowl, using an electric mixer on medium speed, combine butter, cocoa powder, and sugar. The result will be a gritty, chocolate-colored paste. Continue to mix on medium for 1 minute.

Add liquids: Add egg, water, and vanilla to butter mixture. Only mix to combine. Do not overmix.

Make batter: Add dry ingredients. Mix on medium speed until all flour has been incorporated. Fold in chocolate chips.

Bake: Scoop batter into each cup, filling it three-quarters full. Once each cup is filled, place pan in oven. Bake for 12 minutes. Remove pan from oven. Let brownie bites cool for 15 minutes. Remove brownie bites from pan. Serve.

RASPBERRY MUFFINS

A blog offers Rory a job. The owner, Sandy, wants Rory to join the team so badly, she sends her a basket of raspberry muffins, calls her repeatedly, and even sends a creep-show video showing a cardboard cutout of Rory working beside the company logo.

Once Rory relents, locates her lucky outfit, and takes the interview, things change. As Rory talks with Sandy, it becomes clear she walked in with no ideas, no interest, and no energy. When Sandy sits back and takes an objective look at this person she's heard so much about, she realizes Rory doesn't live up to the hype. Sandy makes an excuse and cuts the interview short.

These muffins do live up to the hype! With their tender, cake-like texture and bursts of raspberry flavor, they'll make you want to call Sandy and say, "I'll take the job!"

Ingredients:

1 batch streusel topping

½ c melted butter

2 T freshly squeezed lemon juice

2 t grated lemon zest

1 t vanilla extract

½ c milk

½ c ricotta cheese

2 room-temperature eggs

2 c flour

¾ c sugar

2 t baking powder

½ t salt

1 c rinsed and dried fresh raspberries

1 batch lemon glaze

Streusel Topping

¼ c flour

2 T sugar

1 t grated lemon zest

2 T softened butter

Lemon Glaze

¾–1 c powdered sugar

1 T freshly squeezed lemon juice

1 T milk

Prepare oven and pan: Ensure oven rack is in center position. Preheat oven to 375°F. Add paper muffin liners to a standard size, 12-muffin tin.

Prepare streusel topping: In a small bowl, combine flour, sugar and zest. Cut in butter using a pastry cutter or a fork. Once butter is cut in, massage the remaining flour into the butter pieces by hand. The result will be tiny pea-sized balls. Set aside.

(Continued on next page)

RASPBERRY MUFFINS

(Continued)

Combine liquid ingredients: In a medium bowl or large measuring cup, combine cooled butter, lemon juice, zest, vanilla, milk, and ricotta. Stir with a fork. Add eggs. Stir only until combined. Set aside.

Combine dry ingredients: Combine flour, sugar, baking powder, and salt in a medium bowl. Lightly mix together with a dry fork.

Make batter: Add the liquid mixture to the dry, mixing only until combined. Gently fold in the raspberries.

Bake muffins: Scoop the batter into paper muffin cups until each one is full. Using a spoon, top each cup of batter with 2 teaspoons of streusel topping. Place pan in the oven. Bake for 17–19 minutes. Begin checking muffins after 15 minutes. Test for doneness by inserting a toothpick into the center of one muffin. When it comes out clean, the muffins are fully baked. Remove from oven. Cool to room temperature.

Prepare and apply lemon glaze: In a small bowl combine ¾ cup powdered sugar, lemon juice, and milk. Add additional powdered sugar until desired consistency is achieved. Drizzle glaze onto muffins. Serve.

Makes 12 muffins

CAPPUCCINO MUFFINS

The revival not only brings us back into the lives of the Gilmores. It also lets us experience, once again, what life is like in a small town.

When Luke and Lorelai have a heated argument in the middle of the diner, with customers looking on and listening, no one thinks it's odd or embarrassing. It makes it seem like everyone knows everything about everyone in a small town. What's more, this show makes it seem like that's okay.

Luke and Lorelai are arguing, yes, but Luke still leaves the diner to take his muffins out of the oven at the Dragonfly so Lorelai's guests will have them for breakfast the next day. Even when they're not getting along, he still makes an extra effort to support her.

Luke doesn't mention the flavor of the muffins, but the guess is cappuccino. We're talking about Lorelai here. What else would they be?

Ingredients:

3 T espresso powder

½ c hot water

2½ c flour

1 c sugar

2 t baking powder

½ t salt

2 eggs

½ c evaporated milk

½ c cooled melted butter

¾ c mini chocolate chips

Cream Cheese Topping

8 oz cream cheese

3 T sugar

1 egg yolk

Prepare oven and pan: Ensure oven rack is in center position. Preheat oven to 375°F. Add paper muffin liners to a standard-size 12-muffin tin.

Prepare espresso: Add espresso powder to a small bowl. Add the hot water. Stir until dissolved. Set aside.

Combine dry ingredients: In a medium bowl, add flour, sugar, baking powder, and salt. Set aside.

Combine wet ingredients: Crack eggs into a large bowl. Whisk the eggs gently for a few strokes, until the yolks and whites are combined. Add evaporated milk. Whisk together, gently. Continue whisking while slowly adding the cooled butter and coffee mixture.

Make batter: Add the dry ingredients to the wet. Whisk together until all dry ingredients have been incorporated and no white flour is showing. Take care not to overmix. Fold in chocolate chips.

(Continued on next page)

CAPPUCCINO MUFFINS

(Continued)

Mix cream cheese topping: In a small bowl add cream cheese, sugar, and egg yolk. Using an electric mixer, beat on medium speed until all ingredients are fully blended. Increase speed slightly and continue to beat for 30 seconds to add air to the mixture. Set aside.

Prepare muffins: Fill muffin papers with batter until roughly three-quarters full. Spoon a rounded tablespoon of cream cheese filling onto the batter for each muffin. Using toothpicks or a fork, carefully swirl the cream cheese into the batter, creating a pattern on the top of each muffin.

Bake muffins: Place pan in oven. Bake for 18 minutes. Test for doneness by inserting a toothpick into the center of one muffin. When it comes out clean, the muffins are fully baked. Remove from oven. Let cool for 10 minutes. Serve.

Makes 12 muffins

CONTRIBUTED BY
VALERIE CAMPBELL

CHAMPAGNE TANGO SORBET

After Rory says "goodbye" to Logan, he decides he cannot let her go without a proper send-off. He gathers his secret society brothers. Together for one final time, they invite Rory into their whimsical world, complete with rooftop golf, a midnight screening of Kirk's newest indie film, and a wild ride in a vintage convertible. Finally, they arrive at a tango club.

After Logan takes Rory for a quick, awkward whirl around the dance floor, the two fate-crossed lovers slink off to a private room where they sip champagne and talk about the past—and the future.

The whole crew spends the night in an inn they've rented out. Logan tells Rory she has her own room, but she declines it, preferring to stay with him.

In the morning, after their final night together, Rory and Logan let each other go.

Valerie Campbell created a sorbet recipe to commemorate this scene.

Ingredients:

6 tangerines

¾ c sugar

1 c + 2 T champagne or sparkling white wine, *divided*, plus more for serving

3 c water

½ c freshly squeezed lemon juice

Makes 8–10 servings

Valerie Campbell worked as the Key Set Costumer on Gilmore Girls *and was Costume Supervisor for* Gilmore Girls: A Year in the Life. *Valerie is the author of* The Story and Recipes of Valerie's Cat Eye sCream. *Learn more about Valerie and her adventures in ice cream by visiting valeriescateyescream.com.*

Prepare ice cream maker: Place churning canister in freezer 24 hours prior to churning sorbet.

Make champagne tangerine syrup: Zest all 6 tangerines. In a small saucepan, combine sugar, 1 cup champagne and tangerine zest. Bring to a boil. Continue to boil for 5 minutes. Remove from heat. Strain through a fine-mesh sieve into a bowl to remove zest. Add 3 cups water. Set aside.

Puree tangerines: Remove remaining peel from zested tangerines. Place peeled tangerines in blender. Blend until fruit takes on a puree consistency.

Combine liquids: Add tangerine puree, lemon juice and 2 tablespoons of champagne to the syrup. Place in a container. Cover. Refrigerate overnight then freeze for one hour, no more, before churning.

Churn sorbet: Scoop partially frozen sorbet into the churning canister. Assemble the machine and churn for 20 minutes. Scoop churned sorbet into bowl, loaf pan or metal jar. Cover. Freeze for a minimum of 4 hours.

Serve: Remove sorbet from freezer. If sorbet has been frozen for more than 24 hours, let it sit out for 10–15 minutes until it becomes scoopable. Scoop into a serving bowl. Garnish with mint leaves. Serve.

FAUXDOUGH CAKES

In a show of motherly support, Lorelai accompanies Rory on her trip to New York City. Rory's mission is to report on the phenomenon of people lining up outside various businesses to get the latest clothing or trendy food item.

While Rory begins talking to people in line, collecting intel for her piece, Lorelai punks everyone. Not only does she score the one thing everyone has been waiting in line to get—a Cro-dough Cake—she also hits up a guy at a hot dog cart for some dogs at 7:30 in the morning and rolls out with a coveted pair of sneakers before they're available to the public.

She's still the reigning Lorelai!

This recipe is written with Lorelai's line-cutting style in mind. Skip all the work and the long wait of kneading butter into dough. Let store-bought puff pastry be your insider hookup!

Ingredients:

1 c sugar

⅓ c cinnamon

1 egg

2 t water

2 thawed sheets puff pastry

1 qt oil, for frying

Prepare oven and pan: Ensure oven rack is in center position. Preheat oven to 400°F. Cover a baking sheet with a silicone mat or parchment paper. Set aside.

Prepare cinnamon sugar: In a low-sided bowl, mix sugar and cinnamon. Set aside.

Make egg wash: Crack egg into small bowl. Add water. Mix together until fully combined. Set aside.

Cut dough rings: Lay out puff pastry, unfolding it, if necessary, into one layer. Use a 2½ to 3-inch round biscuit cutter, cookie cutter, or small glass, cut dough into 6–8 rings. Repeat for second batch of dough.

Cut out centers: Using a 1½-inch round biscuit cutter, cookie cutter, or shot glass, cut out the center of each circle, taking care to center the cutter before cutting.

Heat oil: Pour oil into a deep-fryer or stockpot, then heat the oil to 360°–370°F.

(Continued on next page)

FAUXDOUGH CAKES

(Continued)

Set up drying rack: Cover a large plate, countertop or cutting board with 2–3 layers of paper towels. Place a wire rack on the paper towels. This is where the cakes will rest after frying.

Bake rings: Place each ring onto the baking sheet. Lightly brush each one with egg wash. Place in oven and bake for 8 minutes. Rings should have puffed up, but will not look "done." Remove from oven.

Fry rings: Immediately begin frying rings. Place one ring in oil. Fry 1–2 minutes, until outside has taken on a golden color. Use tongs to remove from oil and place on drying rack. Repeat for each ring.

Cover with cinnamon sugar: Once all rings have been fried, dip each one into the cinnamon sugar, taking care to cover the full surface, inside and outside. Serve.

Makes 6–8 fauxdough cakes

BANANA SPLIT

While Rory continues working, interviewing various people on the city streets, Lorelai heads back to their hotel room to relax, watch some TV, and take a nap.

Rory returns several hours later, looking a little shaken and disheveled. She confesses to Lorelai that, in the span of a few hours, she met a man wearing a Wookie suit and had a one-night stand with him. She also admits that her friend "DeeDee" in London is actually Logan.

Lorelai takes in all of the information without any dramatic reaction and consoles Rory by calling room service. She orders two banana splits, thus illustrating the difference between regular wallowing (ice cream only) versus wallowing with a side of guilt after lying to your mother (ice cream plus fruit and lots of toppings).

Ingredients:

2 large bananas

2 scoops vanilla ice cream

2 scoops strawberry ice cream

2 scoops chocolate ice cream

½ c fudge sauce

½ c caramel sauce

⅔ c stemmed and sliced fresh strawberries

6 dollops whipped cream

6 maraschino cherries

2–4 T nut topping

2–4 T sprinkles

Assemble foundation: Peel banana and cut it into two halves along the length. Place the two halves, cut-side in, in an oblong bowl or on a plate. Place one scoop of each ice cream flavor in a line between the two banana halves. Repeat for second banana.

Add toppings: Drizzle the ice creams with fudge sauce and caramel sauce. Distribute fresh strawberry slices. Top each ice cream scoop with a dollop of whipped cream. Top each dollop with a maraschino cherry. Sprinkle chopped nuts and sprinkles. Serve immediately!

Makes 2 banana splits

(Continued on next page)

BANANA SPLIT

(Continued)

Caramel Sauce

2 t vanilla extract

1 c heavy cream

¼ c butter

⅔ c water

2 c sugar

Prepare cream and butter: Stir vanilla into heavy cream. Measure and set out the butter so it's easy to access and ready to use. Set aside.

Boil syrup: Attach a candy thermometer to medium saucepan. Add water to saucepan. Slowly and carefully pour the sugar into the center of the pan, making sure no sugar hits the sides. Do not stir. It's okay if the sugar is in a big pile in the center. Leave the mixture completely untouched. Bring the water and sugar to 345°–350°F over high heat.

Mix caramel sauce: As soon as the target temperature has been reached, add butter and cream. Remove from heat. Stir well to combine. Continue stirring until cooled. This is your caramel sauce!

STRAWBERRY SHORTCAKE

Lorelai is daydreaming about strawberry shortcake when Taylor first mentions the town musical. Always one to volunteer for kooky town events, Lorelai raises her hand when Taylor asks who would like to be an advisor on the board.

The first run-through of the musical illustrates a divide between Lorelai and her beloved neighbors. The scenes she thinks are stupid, they all love. The musical may be a little silly and disjointed, sure. Wouldn't Lorelai of old have appreciated that aspect of it?

While she's sitting there taking page after page of notes, two Broadway stars are acting, singing, and dancing on stage at Miss Patty's. For a small town like Stars Hollow, this is a huge pull! Lorelai seems to not care at all. Has Lorelai lost her joy? Perhaps.

Ultimately, though, the musical helps Lorelai find the path that leads her back to herself.

Ingredients:

2 pints fresh strawberries, stemmed and sliced

¼ c sugar

Shortcakes

2 c flour

2 T sugar

1 T baking powder

¼ t salt

7 T butter, *divided*

¾ c heavy cream

Whipped Cream

2 c cold heavy cream

⅓ c powdered sugar

Macerate strawberries: In a large bowl, combine strawberry slices with sugar. Gently toss to combine. Let sit for 1 hour.

Prepare oven and pan: Ensure oven rack is in center position. Preheat oven to 375°F. Cover a baking sheet with a silicone mat or parchment paper. Set aside.

Make shortcake dough: In a medium bowl combine flour, sugar, baking powder, and salt. Cut in 5 tablespoons of butter. Continue to work butter into dry ingredients by hand until all butter has been incorporated. Add ½ cup heavy cream. If dough is too dry, add additional cream 1 tablespoon at a time until it reaches a rollable consistency.

Roll out dough: Lightly flour the surface of a countertop. Place dough on floured surface. Use a rolling pin to roll out dough to ¾-inch thickness. Use a 2- or 3-inch biscuit cutter to cut dough into circles. Place each circle on the pan, leaving about an inch between them. Reroll dough remnants and continue to cut out circles as often as necessary to use up the remaining dough.

(Continued on next page)

STRAWBERRY SHORTCAKE

(Continued)

Brush shortcakes with butter: In a small saucepan melt the remaining 2 tablespoons of butter. Using a kitchen brush, lightly brush each shortcake with a thin layer of butter.

Bake shortcakes: Place pan in oven and bake for 10–12 minutes. Remove from oven and let cool.

Make whipped cream: Pour cold heavy cream into a deep, medium-sized bowl. Using an electric mixer on high speed, beat cream into stiff peaks. Reduce speed to medium-low and add sugar. Gradually increase speed to high and continue beating until all sugar has been incorporated. Turn off mixer. Set aside.

Assemble shortcakes: Cut shortcakes in half like a bagel. Place bottom half on a small plate or in a bowl. Top with strawberries and strawberry juice. Place the top half of shortcake on strawberries. Add another layer of strawberries, if desired. Top with a dollop of whipped cream. Serve.

Makes 6–8 shortcakes

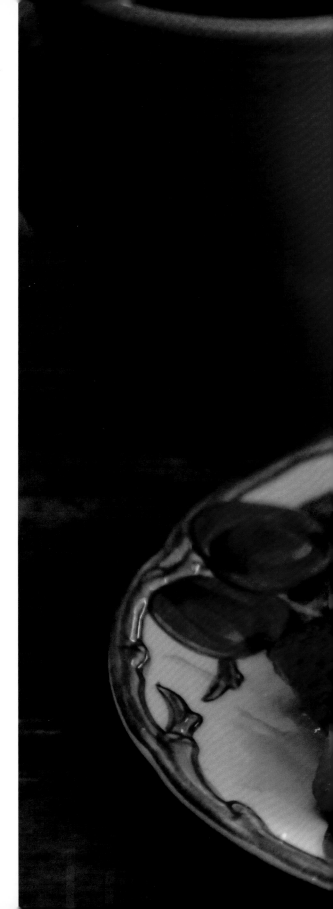

CONTRIBUTED BY
RINI BELL

CRÈME BRÛLÉE

CAST & CREW

"This recipe is the best because it is creamy, not eggy, and crème brûlée is the most fun because there are flames!"

—Rini Bell, "Lulu" in *Gilmore Girls: A Year in the Life*

Ingredients:

2 c heavy cream

3 large eggs

½ c sugar, plus more for the tops

¾ t vanilla extract

8 small navel oranges with pretty peels, *optional*

For 6–8 people

Preheat oven to 250°F.

Heat 2 cups of heavy cream, almost to a simmer. Remove from heat.

In a medium bowl, stir 3 large eggs (this is better than just egg yolks because it's creamier) and ½ cup of sugar with a wooden spoon, just until blended.

Gradually stir in the cream. Begin by stirring in just a few drops, then slowly increase the amount of cream while continuing to stir. If needed, strain through a fine-mesh strainer into a bowl (this will get any eggy parts out).

Stir in the vanilla.

Pour into 6–8 cutey patooty ramekins (or anything similar but the ramekins are the cutest) and put them in a water bath. Set that pan in the oven at 250°F. Bake until the crème brûlées are set but still a little shaky in the middle when they are gently nudged, which is like an hour to an hour and a half. Remove them from the water bath and let them cool to room temp, then cover each one with plastic wrap. Put them in the fridge for 8 hours or up to 2 days.

Best Part: When you are ready to serve them, sprinkle white sugar over the top (the more sugar the more crusty it will be) and blast them with a crème brûlée torch until the sugar turns brown! You will see when you break the surface with a spoon that the texture is crispy at the top, and creamy in the middle :)

Cool Tip: For a French country version, pour the crème brûlée liquid into an orange peel instead of the ramekins. Make sure it is a sturdy peel with no holes, and smaller ones work better in my experience. Slice off the top of the orange—the navel side—then scoop out the insides. Don't put them in a water bath. Use the stem sides of the oranges to balance them on a baking tray. If the stem side is not flat enough for the orange to stand up on its own, slice off a tiny bit of the peel (without creating any holes!) to make it more stable. These will come out more cooked than ones made in ramekins, but they will taste orangey, and be so, so cute!

Rini Bell was born in Rome, Italy, reared in Zurich, Switzerland, and attended the Louise S. McGehee School in New Orleans. Her film and TV credits include Gilmore Girls and Gilmore Girls: A Year in the Life, The Terminal, Bring It On, Ghost World, Reba, Jarhead, King of the Hill, Road Trip, and more. Rini juggles, makes soap (check it out here: etsy.com/shop/BellOfTheBath), and speaks fluent French.

PINK MILKSHAKE

After the book deal with Naomi falls through and the Condé Nast opportunities dry up, Rory moves back to Stars Hollow. She tells everyone, including herself, that it's only temporary, but the older adults around her recognize her situation for what it is: a career slump.

They offer to introduce her to the other thirtysomethings whose careers have been sidelined. They've all formed a sort of "gang" in town, hanging out together regularly.

Rory could not be less interested. When her peers eagerly await even the slightest acknowledgment from her at the town meeting, she avoids making eye contact. When Rory delivers the *Gazette* to Taylor's store and finds them all there with one pink milkshake, she asks about it. When she finds out they're reenacting a scene from a movie, she bolts.

Rory may be thirtysomething, and she may have lost her career momentum, but it's not like her, at all, to fritter away her days. She still has the same work ethic she has always had, to the point she'll take a job running the town newspaper for no pay. She has zero interest in sitting around reenacting pop culture with a bunch of jobless nerds.

She would rather spend her downtime lounging by the pool with her mom.

Ingredients:

4 c vanilla bean ice cream

26 maraschino cherries, 24 with stems removed, 2 with stems intact

¼ c milk

Whipped cream, for serving

Blend milkshake: In blender add ice cream, 24 stemless cherries, and milk. Blend until fully combined, and cherries have all been liquified.

Assemble: Pour milkshake into 2 chilled glasses. Top each with whipped cream and cherry. Serve.

Makes 2 milkshakes

PROFITEROLES

It's the first town meeting we're attending in nearly a decade. There are some new faces, like Donald's! There are some new attitudes, like Taylor's sudden willingness to host an LGBTQ Pride Parade.

However, some things are still exactly the same as they've always been, like Lorelai sneaking in food. This time it is profiteroles, likely purchased from Weston's Bakery.

Let's make these the bakery way—from scratch. They're worth the work!

Ingredients:

1 batch pastry cream filling

1 batch choux pastry shells

1 batch chocolate glaze

Assemble profiteroles: Outfit a piping bag with a sharply pointed tip. Fill piping bag with pastry cream. Pick up one choux pastry shell. Gently poke the piping tip into a side crevice. Slowly squeeze piping bag until pastry shell feels heavy and expands slightly. Return pastry shell to tray. Repeat for each shell.

Glaze profiteroles: Turn each filled pastry upside down and dip into the chocolate glaze. Lift pastry and hold over the glaze for a moment to allow excess to run off. Turn shell upright and return to tray. Repeat for all shells.

Makes 24 profiteroles

(Continued on next page)

PROFITEROLES (Continued)

CHOUX PASTRY SHELLS

1 c flour

½ t salt

1 c water

½ c softened butter

4 eggs, lightly beaten

1 egg

1 t water

Prepare oven and pan: Ensure oven rack is in center position. Preheat oven to 375°F. Cover a baking sheet with a silicone mat or parchment paper. Set aside.

Combine flour and salt: In a small bowl, combine flour and salt. Set aside.

CHOCOLATE GLAZE

2 T butter

6 T 60–75% cacao chocolate chips

1 c powdered sugar

1 T corn syrup

2–3 T milk

Make dough: Pour 1 cup of water into a small saucepan. Add butter. Over medium heat, bring to a boil. Immediately remove from heat. Add flour and salt mixture. Use a wooden spoon or similar to combine. Dough will look lumpy. To smooth it out, return the saucepan to medium-low heat and cook dough for a few seconds. As it cooks, use the wooden spoon to turn the dough several times. Once dough forms a smooth ball, remove from heat. Place dough in a medium bowl. Allow to cool for 1–2 minutes.

Make batter: Using an electric mixer on medium-low speed, mix the dough. Gradually incorporate the beaten eggs. Continue to mix until the batter is smooth. This is your batter.

Bake shells: Outfit a piping bag with a large, open tip. Scoop batter into the piping bag. Pipe 1-inch balls of dough onto the baking sheet, 2 inches apart. Use the back of a wet spoon to round out the tops. Create an egg wash by mixing the remaining egg in a small bowl with 1 teaspoon of water until combined. Use a basting brush to gently brush the egg wash onto the tops of the dough balls. Place baking sheet in the oven. Bake for 23 minutes. Turn off oven and crack open the oven door. Keep the baking sheet in the oven for 2 minutes more, then remove from oven. Let cool to room temperature before adding any filling.

Melt butter and chocolate: In a small saucepan over medium heat, melt together the butter and chocolate chips. Once both are fully melted, stir to combine. Remove from heat. Let cool.

Make glaze: In a medium bowl combine powdered sugar, corn syrup, and 1 tablespoon of milk. Add butter and chocolate mixture. Stir with a spoon to combine, thoroughly. Add milk as needed until desired consistency is achieved. This is your glaze!

PASTRY CREAM FILLING

1 T butter

1 T vanilla extract

4 egg yolks

1 c sugar

¼ t salt

2 c cold milk

4 T cornstarch

1 c cold heavy cream

Prepare ingredients: Measure butter and vanilla into a small bowl or ramekin. Set aside. In a medium mixing bowl, using a fork, lightly beat the egg yolks. Add the sugar and salt. Beat to combine. Set aside.

Heat milk: While milk is still very cold, add cornstarch. This will prevent cornstarch from clumping. Stir until cornstarch is fully dissolved. In a large saucepan, bring milk to a simmer over medium heat. Once milk begins to simmer, bubbles will appear around the edge of the pan. Immediately remove from heat.

Temper the eggs: While vigorously whisking the egg yolk mixture, add 1 tablespoon of hot milk. Continue to whisk. Next, add 2 tablespoons of milk. Whisk. Gradually increase the amount of milk added, while continuing to whisk, until all milk has been incorporated.

Thicken custard: Return mixture to saucepan and bring to a simmer over medium heat, stirring often. When the mixture begins to thicken and bubbles appear around the edges, remove from heat. Immediately add butter and vanilla, stirring to combine. Continue stirring for 2–3 minutes to release heat.

Refrigerate: Pour into a large bowl. Cover with plastic wrap. Placed the plastic directly on top of the custard to prevent the custard from forming a skin. Keep the custard on the counter until it reaches room temperature, then refrigerate for 4 more hours.

Mix pastry cream: In a medium mixing bowl, whip cream with an electric mixer until it forms thick ribbons in the bowl. After custard has been refrigerated for 4 hours, fold whipped cream into custard until thoroughly combined. Cover. Refrigerate until ready to use.

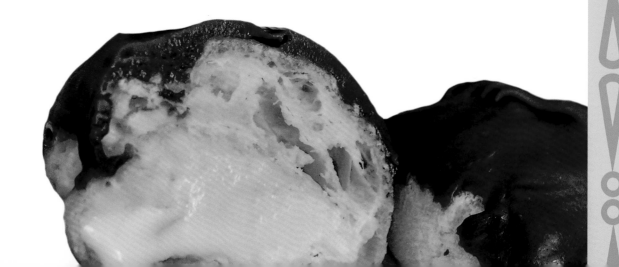

MINI DONUTS

AT HOME

During the "Winter" episode Rory returns to her childhood home. She's eating tacos, mini donuts, two main dishes, and goodness knows what else, so everything seems normal. Then she starts tap dancing her stress away in the middle of the night. What is she stressed about?

She has moved out of her Brooklyn apartment. Her boxes of belongings are scattered to the four winds, divided among everyone close to her. Career-wise, she's still surviving off the fumes of a *New Yorker* article she wrote months earlier. Worst of all, she has no underwear. Rory is in crisis. It's a crisis of career, of identity, and of grief.

At the beginning of the "Winter" episode, she begins the process of shedding her old identity, the Rory everyone has known and loved since the beginning. The people around her have always had a myriad of expectations of that Rory.

Throughout the "Spring" episode, watching her struggle to find work, there's a collective feeling that an upturn is coming, surely. Once the book deal falls through, the "lines" gig evaporates, and even the blog rejects her, it's clear. It's over.

Rory spends her summer regrouping. She stops trying to force things. Instead, she moves home as a means of pressing "reset" on her life.

By the end of "Fall," momentum is building in a new direction. She's living in Stars Hollow, running the town newspaper. She's writing her first novel. With the final four words, we learn she's expecting a child.

As we leave her, Rory is a new version of herself, partly by choice, partly by circumstance, but wholly of her own making. The caterpillar has turned into a butterfly, and we got to witness her metamorphosis—what a gift.

Ingredients:

2¼ c flour, plus more for rolling

½ c sugar

2 t baking powder

1 t baking soda

½ t salt

2 T melted butter

½ c room-temperature milk

1 egg, lightly beaten

1 T vanilla extract

1 qt high-oleic sunflower or vegetable oil

1½ c powdered sugar

Combine dry ingredients: In a medium bowl, combine flour, sugar, baking powder, baking soda and salt.

Combine liquid ingredients: In a small bowl, combine butter, milk, egg, and vanilla.

Make dough: Pour half of liquid ingredients into dry ingredients, mixing with a fork or an electric mixer, to combine. Add remaining liquid ingredients and mix to combine fully until a dough is formed.

Roll out dough: Cover a countertop, prep table, or large cutting board with a light layer of flour. Turn dough out onto the floured surface. Use a rolling pin to roll out dough until it reaches ½-inch thickness.

(Continued on next page)

MINI DONUTS

(Continued)

Cut donuts: Cut dough into circles with a 2-inch diameter. Use a cookie cutter, biscuit cutter, or small glass or dish. Next cut out a ½-inch hole from donut centers by using the bottom end of a piping tip or a sharp paring knife. Reroll all remaining dough to cut additional donuts. Donuts are ready for frying!

Set up drying station: Cover a large plate, countertop, or cutting board with 2–3 layers of paper towels. Place a wire rack on the paper towels. This is where donuts will rest after frying.

Fry donuts: Add oil to deep-fryer or stockpot. If using a pot, insert a candy thermometer. Heat oil to 375°F. Keep oil temperature between 370°F and 380°F. Add donuts, 5 or 6 at a time. Fry for 1 minute. Remove donuts from oil using tongs or frying strainer and carefully place on wire rack in drying station. Repeat until all donuts have been fried.

Add powdered sugar: Pour powdered sugar into a low-sided bowl. Add donuts, one or two at a time. Using a fork, gently toss the donuts around until covered with sugar. Remove. Repeat until all donuts have been covered. Serve.

Makes 30 miniature donuts

GERMAN CHOCOLATE CAKE

In the "Winter" episode, the return to Luke's Diner almost feels like no time has passed at all. Like any authentic small-town diner, it's relatively untouched. Oh, sure, Luke now forbids man buns, and he made new menus featuring Rory's article on the back page. Other than these few minor changes, it's the same as it always was. Thank goodness for that.

Mark your return to your favorite diner by ordering up the top option on the seasonal dessert menu—German Chocolate Cake!

Ingredients:

4 oz German's baking chocolate, chopped

½ c boiling water

3 c cake flour

1 t baking powder

1 t baking soda

⅛ t salt

1 c softened butter

2 c sugar

4 eggs

1 t vanilla extract

¾ c buttermilk

Prepare oven and pans: Ensure oven rack is in center position. Preheat oven to 350°F. Grease and flour two 8-inch round pans and line with parchment paper circles. Set aside.

Melt chocolate: Place chopped chocolate in a small bowl. Add boiling water. Let sit for 2–3 minutes, then stir to combine. Set aside.

Combine dry ingredients: In a medium bowl, combine cake flour, baking powder, baking soda, and salt. Whisk slightly to combine. Set aside.

Cream butter: In a large bowl, combine butter and sugar. Using an electric mixer on medium speed, mix the two until light and fluffy. Add eggs, one at a time, mixing slightly after each. Add vanilla, buttermilk, and chocolate. Only mix long enough to combine.

Make batter: Add the dry ingredients one-third at a time, mixing continuously.

Bake: Ladle batter into the pans, equally. Place pans in oven. Bake for 35–40 minutes. Begin checking after 30 minutes. Check for doneness by inserting a wooden toothpick into the center of one layer. When it comes out clean, the cake is done. Remove from oven. Let cool.

(Continued on next page)

GERMAN CHOCOLATE CAKE

(Continued)

Assemble cake and serve: Once cake layers are room temperature, remove from pan and peel off parchment paper. Add filling. Frost generously. Cut and serve.

Coconut Pecan Filling

1 c evaporated milk

½ c sugar

4 egg yolks

2 T unsalted butter

2 t vanilla extract

1½ c sweetened shredded coconut

½ c coarsely chopped pecans

½ c finely chopped pecans

Make filling: In a medium saucepan, add milk, sugar, and egg yolks. Whisk slightly to combine. Over medium heat, bring to a simmer, with small bubbles appearing around the edge. Remove from heat. Quickly add butter and vanilla, then mix until butter is melted and incorporated. Add coconut and both portions of pecans. Mix fully. Set aside to cool.

German Chocolate Frosting

4 oz German's baking chocolate, chopped

½ c evaporated milk

1 c softened butter

3 c powdered sugar, *divided*

Melt chocolate: Place chopped chocolate into a medium bowl. Set aside. In a small saucepan, heat milk to a simmer. Pour milk over the chocolate pieces. Let sit for 2–3 minutes. Stir to combine. Mixture may look a little grainy—that's okay. Set aside.

Cream butter: In a small bowl, combine butter and 2 cups of powdered sugar. Use an electric mixer to cream the two together.

Make frosting: Gradually add chocolate to the butter mixture, mixing after each addition. Once fully combined, gradually add the final cup of powdered sugar until frosting reaches desired consistency and sweetness.

Makes one 8-inch, 2-layer cake

CONTRIBUTED BY
HEATHER BURSON

CHOCOLATE CAKE

In "Spring," Luke, Lorelai, and all of the favorite townspeople gather at the movie theater to watch a feature film, along with Kirk's latest indie film.

Before the film starts, Kirk stresses the importance of not bringing store-bought food into the theater. While he's talking, the camera pans around to every person in the audience eating store-bought or restaurant-bought food. Luke and Lorelai eat burgers and sip sodas. Hep Alien has half-a-dozen Chinese food containers spread out in front of them. Babette and Morey cook their sausage links on a hibachi grill. It's pandemonium!

Surprisingly, it's Andrew who displays the most amusing disregard for Kirk's warnings when he pulls an entire chocolate cake, complete with birthday candles, out of a bakery box.

Heather Burson created a recipe for Andrew's cake. Here's your chance to recreate the scene with a chocolate cake fit for the movies!

Ingredients:

1⅓ c boiling water

¼ c instant espresso powder

5 oz unsweetened baking chocolate, finely chopped

2 c sugar

⅔ c dark brown sugar

2 c (224 g) cake flour

1 t baking soda

¾ t salt

26 grams unsweetened dark cocoa powder

4 large room-temperature eggs, lightly beaten

⅔ c full-fat sour cream

⅔ c vegetable oil

Prepare oven and pans: Preheat oven to 325°F. Grease and flour three 8-inch round pans and line with parchment paper circles. Set aside.

Melt and sweeten chocolate: In a large mixing bowl, whisk together boiling water, espresso powder, and baking chocolate. Whisk until smooth and chocolate is melted. Add white sugar and brown sugar. Whisk until sugar is dissolved and smooth. Set aside to cool.

Combine dry ingredients: Whisk the cake flour, baking soda, salt, and dark cocoa together in a medium mixing bowl. Set aside.

Mix batter: In a small bowl, whisk together eggs and sour cream until smooth. Add oil and whisk again until well-blended. Add ¼ cup of melted chocolate batter to temper your eggs, whisking vigorously until smooth and blended. Add tempered egg mixture to melted chocolate batter, whisking thoroughly until smooth. Add dry ingredients and whisk again until batter is smooth.

(Continued on next page)

CHOCOLATE CAKE

(Continued)

Pour batter into pans: Divide cake batter evenly between the three prepared cake pans. Give each pan a quick rap on the counter to remove air bubbles.

Bake cake layers: Bake at 325°F for 35–45 minutes, or until a toothpick inserted in the center comes out clean. Allow to cool completely in the pan before removing cake layers. Once cooled, remove layers from pan, peel off parchment paper liner and discard.

Serve: Frost cake generously, as desired. Cut and serve.

Chocolate Frosting

1¼ c room-temperature unsalted butter

¼ c unflavored shortening

80 grams unsweetened dark cocoa powder, sifted

1–1¼ lb powdered sugar, sifted

6–9 T heavy cream

2 t vanilla extract

Pinch salt

Mix frosting: In a large bowl, using an electric mixer, beat butter until smooth and fluffy. Add shortening and beat again. Add sifted cocoa powder and beat on medium speed until dark and smooth. Slowly add powdered sugar 1 cup at a time, alternating with a tablespoon of heavy cream until desired consistency and level of sweetness is reached. Add vanilla and a small pinch of salt. Beat until light and fluffy.

Makes one 8-inch 3-layer cake

Like a real-life Sookie, Heather Burson is the chef/owner of Third Coast Bakery, a full-service bakery and coffee coffee coffeehouse that specializes in creating delicious, allergen-safe baked goods ranging from breads and crackers to elaborate, award-winning wedding cakes. Heather and her bakery are located in Traverse City, Michigan. thirdcoastbakery.com

STRAWBERRY CAKE

At the end of the "Summer" episode, Luke blurts out to Lorelai that she arranged their relationship. She laid out the rules long ago, in the early days, and he's just been going along with her plan this entire time. Lorelai is surprised to hear it, but Luke's words give her a moment of clarity.

All of a sudden, she can see the potentially fatal flaws in their relationship. The reality hits her—if she is ever going to get close to Luke, really close, and truly bond with him as her partner through life, something needs to change. It needs to be something big, and it needs to happen soon.

While all of this is happening, the most lovely, summery strawberry cake sits under the clear cake cover on the counter. Let's let Lorelai worry about her relationship while we focus on the cake!

Ingredients:

1–1½ c thawed frozen strawberries

¾ c milk

1 T strawberry essence or extract, Wild Strawberry Essence from Grasse recommended

2 T high-oleic sunflower or vegetable oil

2–3 drops red food coloring, *optional*

13.5 oz flour

1 T baking powder

½ t salt

1 c room-temperature unsalted butter

13.5 oz sugar

2 eggs

2 egg whites

1 batch strawberry cream frosting

2 c graham cracker crumbs

6–10 fresh, red, ripe, symmetrical, washed strawberries, stems intact

Prepare oven and pans: Ensure oven rack is positioned in center of oven. Preheat oven to 350°F. Use shortening or butter to grease three 8-inch cake pans, then flour the pans. Finally add round pieces of parchment paper to the bottom of each pan. Set aside.

Make strawberry puree: Add thawed strawberries to blender. Blend on medium speed until all berries have liquified. Stop blender and strain puree through a sieve to remove seeds. If resulting puree does not equal ½ cup, repeat process with additional strawberries.

Combine liquids: In a medium bowl, large measuring cup, or jar, combine ½ cup strawberry puree, milk, strawberry essence, oil, and food coloring, if using. Set aside.

Combine dry ingredients: In a separate medium bowl, combine flour, baking powder, and salt. Whisk together. Set aside.

(Continued on next page)

STRAWBERRY CAKE (Continued)

Cream butter: Place butter in a large bowl. Add sugar. Using an electric mixer on medium speed, beat until light and airy. In a small bowl, use a fork to lightly beat eggs and egg whites together. Add the eggs to the butter-and-sugar mixture. Use the mixer to beat until loosely incorporated.

Make batter: While continuing to beat the batter on medium speed, alternate adding ⅓ dry ingredients, with ½ liquid ingredients, then another ⅓ dry ingredients, then the remaining liquids, finally the remaining dry ingredients. Stop the mixer as soon as the final flour addition has been fully incorporated. This is your cake batter.

Bake cake layers: Divide batter into the 3 pans, evenly, about 18 ounces of batter per pan. Gently tap the sides of each pan to flatten out batter. Bake all three pans on center rack in oven for 23–26 minutes. Insert a toothpick into the center of cake to test for doneness. A clean toothpick indicates cake is done. Remove from oven. Let cool, completely. Remove each layer from its pan and peel off the parchment paper. Layers are now ready for assembly.

Assemble cake: Place bottom layer on a cake stand or regular plate. Use a frosting spatula to apply frosting to the top of the layer. Place second layer on top, taking care to place it directly above the bottom layer. Apply frosting. Place top layer on cake. Apply frosting on the top of the top layer, and around sides, using a bench scraper to make the sides smooth.

Decorate cake: By hand, gently apply graham cracker crumbs around the sides of cake. Next cut strawberries in half and position them in a circle, cut-side down, around the top edge of cake. Pipe the plain white frosting in an upside-down cone shape onto the top center of cake. Serve.

Makes one 8-inch, 3-layer cake

Strawberry Cream Frosting

1¾ c cold heavy cream

2 t cornstarch

4 T very soft unsalted butter

⅔ c powdered sugar

½ t strawberry essence

2 T powdered freeze-dried strawberries

Note: Because this is whipped cream–based frosting, wait to prepare this until you are ready to frost your cake. This frosting may only be stored in the refrigerator after it has been used to frost/pipe the cake.

Combine cream and cornstarch: In a deep, medium-sized mixing bowl, combine cold heavy cream and cornstarch. Use a fork to stir until cornstarch is fully dissolved.

Whip cream: Add very, very soft (but not at all melted!) butter to cream. Use an electric mixer on medium speed to begin beating the cream. Once butter has been incorporated, increase speed to high. Continue to whip cream until stiff peaks form.

Add sugar: Reduce speed to medium. Add powdered sugar. Once sugar has been incorporated, increase speed to high and continue to whip until cream has compacted slightly in size and is stiff.

Separate frosting: Outfit a piping bag with a large, open-star tip. Remove ¾ c to 1 cup of frosting from bowl and spoon into piping bag. This will be the white frosting piped onto the top of cake.

Add flavorings: To the remaining frosting add strawberry essence and powdered, dried strawberries. Mix on medium to combine. This is your cake frosting!

CHAMPAGNE CAKE

THE WEDDING

At the end of the "Fall" episode, after a long, sixteen-year wait, it's finally the eve of Luke and Lorelai's wedding. Except, as the happy couple sits at the kitchen table, they realize they cannot wait even a few hours more. Instead, they elope!

Under a full moon in the night sky, wearing a black dress, with Sam Phillips playing their song, Lorelai Gilmore marries Luke Danes.

Afterward, Lorelai drinks Champagne until the sun comes up, then she and Rory utter the fabled final four words.

This cake is a nod to Lorelai, the beautiful bride.

Ingredients:

¾ c milk

½ c champagne or sparkling white wine

2 T high-oleic sunflower or vegetable oil

13.5 oz flour

1 T baking powder

½ t salt

1 c room-temperature unsalted butter

13.5 oz sugar

2 eggs

2 egg whites

1 batch champagne custard filling

1 batch champagne cream frosting

Pretty sprinkles

Prepare oven and pans: Ensure oven rack is positioned in center of oven. Preheat oven to 350°F. Use shortening or butter to grease three 8-inch cake pans, then flour the pans. Finally add round pieces of parchment paper to the bottom of each pan. Set aside.

Combine liquids: In a medium bowl, large measuring cup or jar, combine milk, Champagne, and oil. Set aside.

Combine dry ingredients: In a separate medium bowl, combine flour, baking powder, and salt. Whisk together. Set aside.

Cream butter: Place butter in a large bowl. Add sugar. Using an electric mixer on medium speed, beat until light and airy. In a small bowl, use a fork to lightly beat eggs and egg whites together. Add the eggs to the butter-and-sugar mixture. Use the mixer to beat until loosely incorporated.

Make batter: While continuing to beat the batter on medium speed, alternate adding ⅓ dry ingredients, with ½ liquid ingredients, then another ⅓ dry ingredients, then the remaining liquids, finally the remaining dry ingredients. Stop the mixer as soon as the final flour addition has been fully incorporated. This is your cake batter.

(Continued on next page)

CHAMPAGNE CAKE (Continued)

Bake cake layers: Divide batter into the 3 pans, evenly, about 16 ounces of batter per pan. Gently tap the sides of each pan to flatten out batter. Bake all three pans on center rack in oven for 25–30 minutes. Insert a toothpick into the center of cake to test for doneness. A clean toothpick indicates cake is done. Remove from oven. Let cool, completely. Remove each layer from its pan and peel off the parchment paper. Layers are now ready for assembly.

Assemble cake: Place bottom layer on a cake stand or regular plate. Use a frosting spatula to apply custard filling to the top of the layer. Place second layer on top, taking care to place it directly above the bottom layer. Apply filling. Place top layer on cake. Apply frosting on the top of the top layer, and around sides, using a bench scraper to make the sides smooth.

Decorate cake: By hand, gently apply sprinkles around the sides of cake. Next pipe frosting in round, elegant blobs evenly spaced around the top of cake. Apply a few sprinkles to the piped blobs. Cut cake and serve.

Makes one 8-inch, 3-layer cake

Champagne Custard Filling

8 egg yolks

1½ c Champagne or sparkling white wine

⅓ c sugar (double if using brut)

2 c heavy cream

2 T powdered sugar

Make custard: In a 2- or 3-quart saucepan, combine yolks, sparkling wine, and granulated sugar over medium-high heat, whisking constantly. Continue to heat and whisk until mixture has thickened to a loose pudding consistency. Remove from heat. This is your custard.

Chill custard: Pour custard into a 1-gallon ziplock bag or metal bowl. Fill the kitchen sink, or an oversized bowl with ice. Add water, filling one third. If using a ziplock bag, ensure that the bag is closed securely, then place bag into ice water. If using a bowl, cover, then float bowl in ice bath, taking extra care to not get any water in bowl. Chill this way for 30 minutes, then place in refrigerator for at least 2 hours. Once the custard has set, move on to next step.

Whip cream: In a large, deep mixing bowl, whip the heavy cream to stiff peaks. While continuing to whip, add powdered sugar. Mix until fully incorporated.

Make filling: Fold the whipped cream into the Champagne custard. Mix until fully combined. This is your filling.

Champagne Frosting

1¾ c heavy cream, cold

1 T cornstarch

4 T butter, unsalted, very soft but not melted

¾ c powdered sugar

2 T Champagne or sparkling wine

Note: Because this is whipped cream–based frosting, wait to prepare this until you are ready to frost your cake. This frosting may only be stored in the refrigerator after it has been used to frost/pipe the cake.

Combine cream and cornstarch: In a deep, medium-sized mixing bowl, combine cold heavy cream and cornstarch. Use a fork to stir, until cornstarch is fully dissolved.

Whip cream: Add very, very soft (but not at all melted!) butter to cream. Use an electric mixer on medium speed to begin beating the cream. Once butter has been incorporated, increase speed to high. Continue to whip cream until stiff peaks form.

Add sugar: Reduce speed to medium. Add powdered sugar. Once sugar has been incorporated, increase speed to high and continue to whip until cream has compacted slightly in size and is stiff.

Add champagne: Add the champagne. Mix on medium to combine. This is your cake frosting!

Set up piping bag: Outfit a piping bag with a large, open-star tip. Remove ¾ c to 1 cup of frosting from bowl and spoon into piping bag. This will be the frosting piped onto the top of cake.

RICHARD GILMORE: IN MEMORIAM

When Rory walks into Richard's study, her mind's eye sees him sitting behind his desk. For a moment we can believe he's actually there, just like old times. When her eyes focus on the reality in front of her, the chair behind the desk is empty. The reminder that Richard died several months earlier hits us again and makes a fresh mark.

Throughout the four episodes of the revival, several elements pay homage to him, like the huge portrait of him that Emily orders, which can only signify what an enormous presence Richard Gilmore was.

Thankfully, the "Winter" episode gives us a flashback to the funeral. It's the perfect setting for viewers to feel like we were there and to say "goodbye." It gives us closure.

After the service, we get to see Emily standing beside Richard's coffin, just like M'Lynn stood beside Shelby's coffin in *Steel Magnolias*. Deep in our feelings of grief and sadness, the familiar visual reminds us that life goes on.

Richard's libation of choice, Scotch, makes several appearances throughout *A Year in the Life*, with all three Gilmore women drinking it in multiple scenes. Traditionally Scotch hasn't been a go-to beverage for Lorelai, Rory, or even Emily. Seeing them drink so much of it during the revival can only mean they did it in tribute to Richard.

This section celebrates Richard Gilmore's life with four different Scotch-based cocktails. There's one for each season because that's the kind of person Richard Gilmore was—a man for all seasons.

THE WHIFFENPOOF

IN MEMORIAM

Richard was the consummate entertainer. He loved to fill his house with guests, mix cocktails at his bar cart, watch folks "ooh" and "aah" over the vast array of foods being served, tell stories, drink, dance, and smoke cigars until the wee hours.

We witnessed him in full Party Mode at the Friday Night Christmas Party Lorelai and Rory did not attend. He was dressed to the nines, a little drunk, and thoroughly enjoying some magic moments with friends.

This cocktail adds Scotch to homemade eggnog, a classic for the holidays.

Ingredients:

8 egg yolks

¾ c sugar

3 c milk

1 t vanilla extract

1½ c cold heavy cream

1 c Scotch

Nutmeg, ground or grated, for serving

Make custard: In a medium saucepan, combine egg yolks, sugar, and milk. Measure out vanilla. Set it aside, ready to use. Over medium-high heat, whisk the egg yolks, sugar, and milk together and continue whisking, gently, until the mixture begins to thicken, and bubbles form around the edges. Remove from heat. Quickly whisk in the vanilla.

Add cream and Scotch: Whisk cream into the custard. Once it is fully incorporated, add the Scotch and whisk.

Serve: Pour into glasses or glass mugs. Wait for cream to rise to the top. Sprinkle with nutmeg, if using. Serve warm.

Makes 6 servings

Tip: For a nonalcoholic option, simply omit the Scotch

THE DEBUTANTE

As well-known, respected, and sometimes feared as Richard was in his field and among his peers, he was also an experienced sidekick to Emily, always game to accompany her, whether it was a charity event, a DAR gala, or Rory's coming-out ball. In his patented suit and bow tie, he was always ready to dance, give a toast, or give a roast any time Emily needed him. He knew how important these events were to Emily's happiness, so he did his part to support her.

This cocktail represents the lighter side of Richard's personality—his loving husband side.

Ingredients:

1 c freshly squeezed grapefruit juice

1 c water

½ c sugar

5 oz Scotch

2 oz freshly squeezed lime juice

2 oz peach schnapps or other peach-flavored liqueur

Ice

Lime wedges, for garnish

Make syrup: In a medium saucepan, combine grapefruit juice, water, and sugar over medium heat. Stir to combine. Heat only until sugar has dissolved fully. Remove from heat. Let cool.

Mix cocktail: Pour grapefruit syrup into pitcher or beverage dispenser. Add Scotch, lime juice and peach liqueur. Stir together. Add ice.

Serve: Once the batch is fully chilled, fill small glasses or punch cups with roughly 4 ounces each, omitting ice. Garnish with a lime wedge. Serve.

Makes 6 (4-ounce) cocktails.

THE FRANCHISE

One of Richard's favorite escapes was golf. He thoroughly enjoyed visiting the golf club, hobnobbing with his cronies, and schmoozing into and out of business deals while playing the back nine. The time Richard spent at the club was his time. It was sacred.

Very rarely, he would let others into this world. After some pressure from Emily, he took Rory to the club, gave her her first golf lesson, and talked about her dreams of visiting Fez. He took his new business partner, Jason, and showed him off around the course as a means of recouping some dignity after Jason's father callously booted Richard from the firm.

He even invited Lorelai's new beau, Luke, to play a round of golf. Richard used their time together on the links to persuade Luke to franchise the diner. He was so invested in the idea, he even left Luke some franchise money in his will.

His approach may have seemed a little heavy-handed, but his intentions were pure. Richard wanted to make sure Lorelai had a solid partner and would be secure, even after her father was gone.

Ingredients:

Ice

2 oz Scotch

2 oz elderflower liqueur

8 oz cold ginger beer

Maraschino cherries, for serving

Blend: Add ice to a blender until it is halfway full. Add Scotch and elderflower liqueur. Blend until the ice has broken down and taken on a slushy consistency.

Make cocktail: Spoon icy mixture into two glasses. Add 4 ounces of ginger beer to each glass. Gently stir to combine.

Serve: Top with a cherry, if using. Serve.

Makes 2 cocktails

THE GODFATHER

IN MEMORIAM

Richard Gilmore spent his life surrounded by women—his mother, his wife, his daughter, and his granddaughter. He took his role as the only male in the family quite seriously. To make his mother proud, he did well at Yale, then graduated into the world of big business. Soon he found himself making enough money to buy a grand home and lavish his wife with anything she wanted.

The day his daughter was born, he made a small investment in her name. By the time she was ready to open her own business, the money was there, thanks to Richard's foresight.

He paid for Rory's education, first Chilton, then Yale, until her father took over the responsibility.

Richard Gilmore took care of the women he loved. He was the head of the family. The provider. The final say. The Godfather.

Ingredients:

Ice

1 oz Scotch

1 oz amaretto

Maraschino cherries, for serving

Mix cocktail: Fill a highball glass half with ice. Add Scotch and amaretto. Gently stir. Add cherries. Serve.

Makes 1 cocktail

INDEX

A

Abdoo, Rose, 96–97

agave nectar
  Hot Dog Cart, 83

aioli
  Burger Day, 73–74

aji chili paste
  Salchipapas, 81

allspice
  Glögg, 3
  Swedish Meatballs, 105–106
  Sweet Potato Peanut Stew, 97

almonds
  Glögg, 3

amaretto
  Godfather, 187

anise
  Glögg, 3

apple
  Finger Sandwiches, 55–58

apple cider vinegar
  Burger Day, 73–74

apricots, dried
  Fat-Free Granola, 37

avocado
  Shrimp & Dips, 19–20
  BLT Sandwich, 45

B

bacon
  BLT Sandwich, 45
  Burger Day, 73–74
  Migas, 109–110
  NYC Burger, 69–70
  Tortilla Española, 25

baking chocolate
  Chocolate Cake, 167–168
  German Chocolate Cake, 163–165

baking powder
  Cappuccino Muffins, 131–132
  Champagne Cake, 175–177
  German Chocolate Cake, 163–165
  Mall Pretzels, 33–34
  Mini Donuts, 157–158
  Raspberry Muffins, 127–128
  Strawberry Cake, 171–173
  Strawberry Shortcake, 145–146

baking soda
  Brownie Bites, 125
  Chocolate Cake, 167–168
  German Chocolate Cake, 163–165
  Mall Pretzels, 33–34
  Mini Donuts, 157–158

balsamic vinegar
  Sammies, 47–49

banana
  Banana Fudge Milkshake, 121–122
  Banana Split, 141–142

Banana Fudge Milkshake, 121–122

Banana Split, 141–142

basil
  Italian Street Pizza, 51–52
  Linguine & Meatballs, 101–102
  Sammies, 47–49

Basket of Fries, 79

beans, black
  Tater Tot Tacos, 41–42

béarnaise sauce
  NYC Burger, 69–70

beef base
  Poutine, 77

beef bouillon
  Poutine, 77

beef broth

C

cabbage
    Hot Dog Cart, 83–85
cake
    Champagne Cake, 175–177
    Chocolate Cake, 167–168
    German Chocolate Cake, 163–165
    Strawberry Cake, 171–173
Campbell, Valerie, 135
Cappuccino, 5
Cappuccino Muffins, 131–132
Caprese Sandwich, 49
Caramel Sauce, 142
cardamom
    Glögg, 3
carrot
    Hot Dog Cart, 84
    Linguine & Meatballs, 101
    Shepherd's Pie, 115
cauliflower
    Sweet Potato Peanut Stew, 97
cayenne pepper
    Crab Balls, 27
    Lobster Mac 'n' Cheese, 93
celery
    Linguine & Meatballs, 101
    Shepherd's Pie, 115
cereal
    Fat-Free Granola, 37
Champagne
    Champagne Cake, 175–177
    Champagne Tango Sorbet, 135
Champagne Cake, 175–177
Champagne Custard Filling
    Champagne Cake, 176
Champagne Frosting
    Champagne Cake, 177
Champagne Tango Sorbet, 135
cheddar cheese

Burger Day, 73, 74
    Finger Sandwiches, 56
    Fondue, 31
    Shepherd's Pie, 115
    Tater Tot Tacos, 41
cheese
    Migas, 109–110
    Tater Tot Tacos, 41
cheese curds
    Poutine, 77
chicken
    Chicken Scaloppine, 99
    Finger Sandwiches, 55–56
    Parmesan Cutlets, 89–90
chicken broth
    Poutine, 77
    Swedish Meatballs, 105–106
chicken cutlet
    Sammies, 49
    Chicken Scaloppine, 99
chili
    Hot Dog Cart, 84
chili powder
    Hot Dog Cart, 84
    Tater Tot Tacos, 41
    Chipotle Cream, 41
chipotle sauce
    Tater Tot Tacos, 41
chocolate
    Banana Fudge Milkshake, 121–122
    Chocolate Cake, 167–168
chocolate chips
    Brownie Bites, 125
    Cappuccino Muffins, 131–132
    Profiteroles, 153–155
Chocolate Frosting
    Chocolate Cake, 168
chocolate glaze
    Profiteroles, 153–154

Fondue, 31
food coloring
    Strawberry Cake, 171
Franchise, 184
freeze-dried blueberries
    Fat-free Granola, 37
freeze-dried strawberries
    Strawberry Cake, 173
French bread
    French Bread Pizza, 61
    Garlic Bread, 17
French Bread Pizza, 61
French fries
    Basket of Fries, 79
    Poutine, 77
    Salchipapas, 81
Fudge Sauce, 122

G

garlic
    Beef Bulgogi, 113
    Finger Sandwiches, 55
    Garlic Bread, 17
    Linguine & Meatballs, 101
    Migas, 109
    Poutine, 77
    Swedish Meatballs, 105
    Tater Tot Tacos, 41–42
German Chocolate Cake, 163–165
German Chocolate Frosting, 165
Gimlet, 13
Gin Martini, 11
ginger
    Beef Bulgogi, 113
    Burger Day, 73
    Finger Sandwiches, 55
    Glögg, 3
ginger beer
    Franchise, 185

Glögg, 3
gochujang
    Beef Bulgogi, 113
Godfather, 187
graham cracker crumbs
    Strawberry Cake, 171–172
granola
    Fat-Free Granola, 37
grapefruit juice
    Debutante, 183
green chilis
    Fondue, 31
green onion
    Beef Bulgogi, 113
    Fluke Carpaccio, 23
ground beef
    Burger Day, 73–74
    Hot Dog Cart, 84
    Linguine & Meatballs, 101–102
    London Burger, 65
    NYC Burger, 69
    Shepherd's Pie, 115
    Swedish Meatballs, 105
ground lamb
    Shepherd's Pie, 115
ground pork
    Swedish Meatballs, 105
ground sirloin
    Burger Day, 73–74
Gruyere
    Lobster Mac 'n' Cheese, 93

H

half-and-half
    Lobster Mac 'n' Cheese, 93
ham
    Finger Sandwiches, 56
    Tortilla Española, 25
Havarti cheese

Profiteroles, 153–155
prosciutto
    Sammies, 47
Prosciutto Provolone Panini
    Sammies, 47
provolone
    Sammies, 47
puff pastry
    Fauxdough Cakes, 137
    quinoa flakes
    Fat-Free Granola, 37

R

Rachel Sandwich, 48
raisins
    Finger Sandwiches, 55–56
    Glögg, 3
raspberries
    Raspberry Muffins, 127–128
    Raspberry Muffins, 127–128
red bell pepper
    Sweet Potato Peanut Stew, 97
red wine
    Glögg, 3
    Linguine & Meatballs, 101–102
    Sangria, 9
    Shepherd's Pie, 115–116
Reference Guide, xi
relish
    Hot Dog Cart, 83
    Sammies, 48
Reuben Sandwich, 48
rice
    Beef Bulgogi, 113
ricotta cheese
    Raspberry Muffins, 127–128
Ristretto, 7
roast beef
    Finger Sandwiches, 57

Roast Beef with Horseradish Cream
    Finger Sandwiches, 57
rolled oats
    Fat-Free Granola, 37
rum
    Sangria, 9
Russian Dressing, 48
    Salchipapas, 81

S

salsa
    Migas, 109–110
Sammies, 47–49
Sangria, 9
sauerkraut
    Sammies, 48
Scotch
    Debutante, 183
    Franchise, 185
    Godfather, 187
    Whiffenpoof, 181
serrano pepper
    Finger Sandwiches, 55
    Fluke Carpaccio, 23
sesame oil
    Beef Bulgogi, 113
    Fluke Carpaccio, 23
sesame seeds
    Beef Bulgogi, 113
    Burger Day, 73
shallot
    London Burger, 65–66
    NYC Burger, 69
    Poutine, 77
    Shepherd's Pie, 115
Shepherd's Pie, 115–116
sherry
    Chicken Scaloppine, 99
    Finger Sandwiches, 55

CONVERSION CHARTS

Metric and Imperial Conversions

(These conversions are rounded for convenience)

Ingredient	Cups/Tablespoons/Teaspoons	Ounces	Grams/Milliliters
Butter	1 cup/16 tablespoons/2 sticks	8 ounces	230 grams
Cheese, shredded	1 cup	4 ounces	110 grams
Cornstarch	1 tablespoon	0.3 ounce	8 grams
Cream cheese	1 tablespoon	0.5 ounce	14.5 grams
Flour, all-purpose	1 cup/1 tablespoon	4.5 ounces/0.3 ounce	125 grams/8 grams
Flour, whole wheat	1 cup	4 ounces	120 grams
Fruit, dried	1 cup	4 ounces	120 grams
Fruits or veggies, chopped	1 cup	5 to 7 ounces	145 to 200 grams
Fruits or veggies, puréed	1 cup	8.5 ounces	245 grams
Honey, maple syrup, or corn syrup	1 tablespoon	0.75 ounce	20 grams
Liquids: cream, milk, water, or juice	1 cup	8 fluid ounces	240 milliliters
Oats	1 cup	5.5 ounces	150 grams
Salt	1 teaspoon	0.2 ounce	6 grams
Spices: cinnamon, cloves, ginger, or nutmeg (ground)	1 teaspoon	0.2 ounce	5 milliliters
Sugar, brown, firmly packed	1 cup	7 ounces	200 grams
Sugar, white	1 cup/1 tablespoon	7 ounces/0.5 ounce	200 grams/12.5 grams
Vanilla extract	1 teaspoon	0.2 ounce	4 grams

Oven Temperatures

Fahrenheit	Celsius	Gas Mark
225°	110°	¼
250°	120°	½
275°	140°	1
300°	150°	2
325°	160°	3
350°	180°	4
375°	190°	5
400°	200°	6
425°	220°	7
450°	230°	8